D1013343

*Making the Most of 9 Surprising Trends that Can Benefit Your Church*

# GIANT AWAKENINGS

## THOM S. RAINER

BROADMAN
& HOLMAN
PUBLISHERS

Nashville, Tennessee

© 1995
by Thom S. Rainer
All rights reserved
Printed in the United States of America
4261-73


0-8054-6173-6
Dewey Decimal Classification: 269
Subject Heading: RELIGIOUS AWAKENING
Library of Congress Card Catalog Number: 94-23668
Unless otherwise noted, all Scripture quotations are from the Holy
Bible, New International Version, copyright ©1973, 1978, 1984 by
International Bible Society.


**Library of Congress Cataloging-in-Publication Data**

Rainer, Thom S.
   Giant awakenings: making the most of 9 surprising trends that can benefit
your church / by Thom S. Rainer
   p.   cm.

   ISBN 0-8054-6173-6

   1. Pastoral theology.  2. Church renewal.  3.Church growth—United States.
4. Twenty-first century — Forecasts.  I. Title.
   BV4011.R34      1995
   269—dc20
                                                          95-23668
                                                          CIP

To Nan Rainer, my mother,
A mama of love and a lady of dignity
and grace in the most difficult of days.

Sam S. Rainer, Jr., my brother.
I have always looked up to you; I always will.

And always to Jo, my wife,
more beautiful today than our
first date in 1972.

*Giant Awakenings* by Thom Rainer is a significant, well informed, and well written analysis of important trends that will shape the life and ministry of the church as we move into the twenty-first century. Rainer's keen analysis and insightful treatment of these timely and pressing concerns is not only substantive reading, this is *must* reading for all pastors and church and denominational leaders.

—David S. Dockery, vice-president of
Academic Administration, The
Southern Baptist Theological Seminary

Thom Rainer has a fresh and realistic view of the trends that are affecting the traditional church. *Giant Awakenings* offers you, the pastor, true growth tactics for the traditional church and shows you how to apply these principles to your church without the necessity of turning you or your church into something that neither of you profess to be.

—Dr. Larry Gilbert, chairman,
Ephesians Four Ministries (parent
organization of Church Growth
Institute and Sunday School Dynamics)

No one understands the current state of the church like Dr. Thom Rainer. Let me recommend you read the nine conclusions of Dr. Rainer in his book, *Giant Awakenings*. You will come away blessed and encouraged that God is indeed desiring to do great things in our midst.

—Dr. Mark S. Hearn, pastor, Grace
Baptist Church, Evansville, Indiana

This is a book I have been waiting for. Far too long the church that seeks to grow has been fed on nothing but methodology. Methods are important and have their place, but they are effective when undergirded by the essential *spiritual* and *biblical* principles that always must be there if growth is to be lasting and God honoring. This book seeks to bring these biblical principles to bear on church growth approaches—and does it very well.

—Dr. Lewis A. Drummond, Billy
Graham professor of evangelism and
church growth, Beeson Divinity School
of Samford University

# Contents

# Preface

WHAT IS GOING ON OUT THERE? For years I have heard that question asked by pastors, church staff, and inquiring laypeople. Knowing that I write about churches, consult with churches, and teach about churches, some have waited for my response to the question about churches in our nation. These men and women have a heart to reach people for Christ, but they are confused about the directions of both the church and the society in which we live. Many different voices seem to be giving different and sometimes contradicting advice.

For over one year I studied churches of different denominations, sizes, worship styles, and locations. I visited some, wrote some, and talked with many on the telephone. I also spoke with denominational leaders, other church consultants, and academic leaders, all of whom had regular contact with a variety of churches. I did not approach these various resources with a well-planned, sociologically-correct set of questions. I simply desired to find out, "What's going on out there?"

After months of copious note taking and listening, I noticed some major trends emerging from my conversations. But I did not desire just to look at the "latest happenings." I also wanted to put the prospective future of the churches in a historical context. History is often cyclical, so I viewed the possible trends from the broader perspective of two thousand years of church history.

Many of my conclusions were nothing like my initial perspectives. Because of the high degree of subjectivity of my study, I went over my conversations and historical information again and again. I can never be fully satisfied that I made my conclusions free of bias and errors. But what you are about to read is, to the best of one fallible person's judgment, nine major trends for the American church in the twenty-first century.

Before I wrote the manuscript I realized that my conclusions implied that many of the elements typically associated with "traditional" churches were those that would be renewed and refocused in the years to come. Indeed, as many pastors and other staff members shared with me, the beleaguered and often-criticized traditional church may very well be making a "comeback" of major proportions in the twenty-first century.

I invite you to read about these trends with an open and prayerful heart. They represent movements that could be "giant awakenings" in the years ahead. And somewhere in the midst of these words, I pray that you will find some information that could be of benefit to you and your church. Thank you for inviting me to your time of reading and study. I pray that God will bless you immeasurably as you seek His awakenings in your own church.

# Acknowledgments

I THOUGHT I WOULD BE A PASTOR the rest of my life. Then an unexpected call came from Louisville, Kentucky. Would I be willing to be considered for dean of a new graduate school at The Southern Baptist Theological Seminary? With a miraculous set of events in a whirlwind of time, I heard God's voice saying, "Go." Today I write with a humble and grateful heart for this exciting opportunity. In this position I am able to teach and write about the topics I love: evangelism, missions, and church growth. I am thankful to God for my alma mater and employer, Southern Seminary.

Within this institution I express particular gratitude to President Al Mohler and Vice President David Dockery of the seminary. Their encouragement and inspiration have been motivational forces for my writing ministry. A special word of thanks goes to a special group at the seminary, the dean's council: David Dockery (School of Theology); Diana Garland (Church Social Work); Lloyd Mims (Church Music); and Dennis Williams (Christian Education).

I consider myself blessed to be the dean of the Billy Graham School of Missions, Evangelism, and Church Growth for many reasons. One of my major reasons for gratitude is that I get to serve with the greatest faculty on earth: Mark Terry, David D'Amico, Bryant Hicks, Hal Poe, Bob Hughes, Jim Chancellor, and John Dever. Thank you, colleagues, for the team spirit and Christlike spirit you demonstrate.

A very special word of gratitude goes to Robin Ebeyer who typed every word of the manuscript . . . again and again. Robin is my secretary and a very important person in the Graham School. Her willing and cheerful spirit is a tremendous asset to me and to the school.

Forrest W. Jackson of Broadman & Holman has once again proved to be an outstanding editor and good friend. This work is my second book with Forrest, whose abilities I appreciate more with each passing day.

From the first day I began writing this book, I heard the prayers of my three sons for its completion and blessings by God. It is humbling to know that my sons walk closer to the Savior than I do myself. Thank you, Sam, Art, and Jess. You make your dad so very proud.

How does one express gratitude to a wife who loves, gives, works, and prays for an undeserving husband? My wife, Jo, *does* deserve my deepest thanks for proofreading this book, for taking household responsibilities that should have been my own, and for encouraging me when my patience was thin and my body was weary. But more than all of this, Jo provides an atmosphere of love and joy that allows me to work at my best. No husband could possibly be as blessed as I. To you, Jo, with a heart full of love, I say a thousand thank you's.

# Introduction

# The Premature Obituary

The report of my death was an exaggeration.

—Mark Twain, in a cable from Europe to the Associated Press

MEET RON HUTCHINS. Ron is the pastor of First Baptist Church in Red River, Alabama. First Baptist recently celebrated its 150th anniversary in the small, rural community of 1,600 people.

Ron loves the church, the community, and his ministry to both. His nine-year tenure at First Baptist has not always been smooth, but for the most part, it has been fulfilling.

In recent months, however, the pastor has become concerned. Though Ron believes he has done a credible work at the church, he still has questions. Could he do more? Is the church doing the ministry God has called her to do? Are there changes that should be implemented? Is he as a pastor, moving too rapidly? Is he moving too slowly?

Ron is aware of the many voices speaking about the church in America. "The church must undergo radical change to be effective!"; "Market the church for evangelistic results!"; "Marketing the church is unbiblical!"; "The church must accommodate the baby boomers!"; "The church is accommodating culture too much!"; "Contemporary music must be a part of your worship services!"; "The small church is dead!"; and on and on . . .

The multiple voices are confusing, to say the least. On this muggy day in July, Ron visits a Christian book store. He reads the back cover of a new book about the church. Of all the voices he hears, this one is the most disturbing. The back cover reads: "Before long, traditional churches will be nothing more than cuddly, sentimental creatures who are studied primarily as skeletons in the halls of a museum."

Could it be possible? Is the traditional church in America a relic of the past? And, if so, what can Ron do about First Baptist? He knows several pastors who tried to implement significant change in their traditional churches. Some of them were fired. Others saw the life and unity of these churches disrupted to the point of chaos.

Pastor Ron Hutchins is confused. Intuitively (or perhaps hearing the voice of the Spirit) he knows that the good people of First Baptist could not handle the massive change suggested by many "experts." Yet he desires intensely for the church to be a vital instrument for God's Kingdom. Where does he go from here?

## The Confusion That Reigns

We live in a confusing time. The pace of change is accelerating. The average American cannot assimilate all the changes taking place around him or her. And the average church member, particularly in a traditional church, sees the church as a refuge from the maddening world and its frantic pace.

But many pundits are claiming that the traditional church is no longer an effective instrument for the Kingdom. With as many as 95 percent of churches in the United States classified as traditional, church leaders and pastors like Ron Hutchins represent the majority of church leaders in America today. Yet many of these leaders are confused. "Change the church!" the voices exclaim. But, the very change instituted to make the church more effective often becomes the chief source of demoralization and ineffectiveness. Ron Hutchins feels like his situation is a catch-22. He thinks he must choose between an ineffective status quo or a demoralizing infusion of change which too will render the church ineffective.

## The Myth of the Dinosaur

I must confess that I too once wondered if the traditional church was a dinosaur, a creature headed toward extinction. But, for over one year, I contacted or visited nearly two hundred churches of various sizes, denominations, worship styles, and ministry approaches. I classified the churches as either traditional or nontraditional (See my definition of the traditional church in this chapter). I examined the growth rates, conversion rates, and opinions of leaders in the churches. The results of my study surprised me: *There was virtually no correlation between the growth and outreach of the church and the type of church—traditional or nontraditional.* Actually, the traditional church had a slightly higher conversion rate than the nontraditional church.

Now some may find fault with my conclusion. The "universe" for the study was relatively small. And the classification of traditional and nontraditional may have been somewhat arbitrary. I admit that my study was not the ideal for most sociologists, statisticians, and demographers. Yet my conclusion has not changed in the months since the study. I continue to find that other factors are more positively correlated to growth and ministry than the traditional or nontraditional classification of the church: location, prayer ministries, pastoral longevity, outreach ministries, and others. Plus my voice is not the only one speaking. In this book you will meet other Christian leaders who also believe that the best days of the traditional church are just ahead.

The use of hymnals, traditional 11:00 A.M. services, Sunday School programs, and in-depth expository preaching do nothing to detract from the effectiveness of a church's ministry. To the contrary, some of the traditional methodologies actually enhance effectiveness.

## Change and the Traditional Church

I am not advocating that the traditional church should never change. To be effective the church must constantly seek to understand its culture and make methodological changes when necessary. Change is inevitable. Rather, I am concerned about the *types* of changes implemented.[1] Many leaders have unwisely accepted the myth of the dinosaur and introduced changes to areas that still have tremendous value. This "devaluation of the church's character" (which will be discussed more fully later) means that the church has been stripped of their its heritage and identity to the point that effective ministry is all but impossible.

## Going Against the Grain

Some of the better-selling books on the church have focused on innovative, contemporary ministries—churches that do not use hymnals, have no religious symbols, and have an extensive cell-group ministry. Now I do not find fault with the message of these books. We *should* praise God for the evangelistic successes of these nontraditional church models.

The problem, however, is the implicit conclusion that to be effective, a church must be nontraditional. But, as you will discover in this book, effective traditional models abound. Indeed, the thesis of this book goes against the grain of some user-friendly approaches and nontraditional-only models advocated today. *The traditional church in the twenty-first century will not only survive, but it will experience a profound renewal and revival.* Such a prediction may seem bold to some and foolish to others. But, as you read through this book, I pray that you will see some of the "mercy drops" that are preceding a potential "showers of blessings."

## A Word About the Nontraditional Church

*Giant Awakenings* is a positive book about traditional churches. It is *not* a negative assessment of nontraditional churches. My primary concern is that, in our infatuation with newer models of ministry, we have failed to see how God is blessing numerous traditional churches and long-standing models.

The Kingdom of God is large enough for both models and the multitude and variety of ministry expressions within each large category. I will continue to read eagerly about nontraditional church models. And I will continue to learn from these newer models. Neither "traditional" nor "nontraditional" carry negative or positive connotations throughout this book. They are both evaluated in light of their biblical faithfulness and ministry effectiveness.

## Defining the Traditional Church

Before we proceed, a definition of the traditional church is in order. Most of us recognize a traditional church when we see one, although we have difficulty giving it a precise definition. We even recognize that some churches are "more" traditional than others. When I asked several Christians from both traditional and nontraditional churches to describe their perception of the traditional church, they offered the following characteristics. They said that the traditional church tends to:

- design ministries around ongoing programs, many of which are denominationally originated (a program-based church).

- utilize Sunday School as their primary small-group and Bible-teaching ministry.

- have one or two Sunday morning services as their primary time of corporate worship.

- emphasize personal contacts to church visitors as a primary means of outreach.

- embrace a confrontational model of evangelism.

- use hymns and hymnbooks in their worship services.

- have laity involved in both church administration and ministry.

- have well-established relationship patterns.

- be older than ten years.

- have a greater resistance to change than nontraditional churches.

While these are valid observations, they miss the true heartbeat of many established churches. The word "tradition" implies that a set of values is handed down and carried forward from generation to generation. Certainly some of those values include such traditional methodologies as the use of hymnbooks and Sunday School. Yet these methodologies are but instruments for a far more important agenda.

The heart of the traditional church is the carrying forward from generation to generation of two important values: the unchanging truths of the Christian faith and a sense of family and community. If anything of significance has been lost in some of the efforts to make the church relevant to contemporary society, it has been these two values.

The first value, the unchanging truths of the Christian faith, concerns doctrine. Robert Wuthnow, director of the Center for the Study of American Religion at Princeton University, is foremost among the social scientists studying the church as it heads toward a new millennium. His primary concern about nontraditional churches is the issue of doctrine. Speaking of the small-group movement in these churches, Wuthnow laments that "they do little to increase the biblical knowledge of their members. Most of them do not assert the value of denominational traditions or pay much attention to the distinctive theological arguments that have identified variants of Christianity or Judaism in the past."[2] Though cardinal Christian doctrines such as love, mercy, and forgiveness are prevalent in these churches, the full testimony of Scripture is skewed and incomplete. "Gone is the God of judgment, wrath, justice, mystery, and punishment. Gone are concerns about the forces of evil. Missing . . . is a distinct interest in heaven and hell, except for the small heavens and hells that people experience in everyday lives."[3]

Not all nontraditional churches, however, are "atheological." Wuthnow's warning is for those churches where doctrine has become peripheral. As Os Guiness stated in his critique of the Church Growth Movement, the church that does not pass down the tradition of doctrine is the church headed for extinction, the church with "no grand-children."[4]

It is the tradition of doctrine that the established church has carried well from generation to generation. One of the primary reasons for the success and tenacity of the Sunday School for over two centuries has been its emphasis on teaching the total of biblical revelation to all age groups. Graded Sunday Schools are more than just another methodology; they are vital instruments for communicating and teaching doctrine to all generations.

The expository sermon, a characteristic of many traditional churches, has likewise been an integral force in the handing down of doctrine to successive generations. Application and relevance to everyday living have not been avoided in these sermons. The first focus, however, has been upon teaching doctrine through the biblical text, with application and relevance following.

The key element of tradition is the sense of family and community that the established church conveys. Wuthnow cites Bellah when he refers to the church as a "community of memory."[5] Many sources of rich narrative tradition are experiencing tremendous pressures of change: ethnic groups, families, and residential communities. The traditional church has had and continues to have the opportunity to be a bearer of those rich traditions that may otherwise be lost. The very identity of being a Christian has been nurtured in many of the established churches. And, in the sense that the same identity has been adopted by other church members, the traditional church becomes a community, a home, and a family. How desperately we need such a community in our transient, changing society!

Such, then, are two important definitional phrases of the traditional church: a bearer of doctrine and a community of memory. Many of the other identifying characteristics of the established church are but instruments used in the context of these defining factors.

Many churches have elements of both the traditional and non-traditional, yet over 90 percent of churches tend to be more traditional than not. Is God done with all these churches? To the contrary, I believe the obituaries written about these churches are definitely premature. Let us look at some of these death predictions.

## Some Premature Obituaries

Though the following obituaries are not necessarily about the traditional church per se, they are typically associated with an established church. These are the six most-frequently-mentioned death predictions.

### Premature Obituary #1: The Small Church Will Disappear within Twenty Years

The post-World-War II era saw a massive population shift to the suburbs. Along with this phenomenon came the growth of new suburban churches, some of which eventually became megachurches. Unfortunately for smaller churches—both in the city and rural areas—most of the growth in megachurches came at the expense of the smaller churches rather than from the unchurched and non-Christian population. Consequently, some observers proclaimed the impending demise of the small church.

The suburban flight trend, however, is diminishing. On the horizon is an influx of people back to small towns and rural areas. In the first three years of the nineties decade, 64 percent of nonmetropolitan counties experienced population growth.[6] Americans who moved to the smaller communities did so for affordable housing, a better quality of life, and a less-frantic pace.[7] Smaller churches will attract many of these wearied people who desire a simpler, more intimate lifestyle.

Leonard Sweet notes that "people are moving to small towns because of atmosphere, lower taxes, smaller more responsive and safer school districts, and so on."[8] He sees this demographic movement as an extraordinary opportunity for traditional churches: "What a tremendous moment in history for churches to be on the breaking edge of this change, especially old-line denominations whose majority of churches are in small towns across America."[9]

Yet Sweet warns that small-town churches must be prepared to meet this population shift if they are to reach the new "penturbians." I believe that many of these small-town churches, which are largely traditional by definition, will reap a harvest from these relocated persons. Exciting opportunities for reaching a new demographic segment abound.

### Premature Obituary #2: The Program-Based Church Is a Relic of the Past

A major reason to rejoice in the life of the church in the late twentieth century is the unleashing of the laity for ministry. Greg Ogden calls this renewed emphasis "The New Reformation."[10] A worldwide movement of God is taking place where the work of ministry is being shifted from the clergy to the laity.

One of the expressions of the New Reformation is ministry done outside the realm of a church's established programs. For example, one lay person in a church I pastored sensed a call from God to provide a food ministry for the many indigents in another section of the city. That ministry is now one of the largest in the state. The church did not have an established food program or ministry, so this woman was given permission by the leadership of the church to initiate the process herself.

Partly because of the great number of laity-initiated ministries, some pundits have declared that program-based ministries are fast becoming a relic of the past. Others see the small-group movement replacing the functions of the program-based church. This conclusion is again part of the "either/or" syndrome prevalent today. Either you have laity-initiated ministries or you have programs. Either you have small groups or you have programs. Why must one facet of the church's ministry die (programs) when another is introduced (e.g. laity-initiated ministries)? Instead of "either/or," why not "both/and"?

Actually, in even the most nontraditional models, program ministries usually are present. For example, I visited a nontraditional church where the pastor declared that programs were no longer a part of the church's ministry. Yet, when I read a church brochure, I discovered they had an ongoing class of spiritual-gifts discovery which utilized the material of a well-known megachurch. The church did have a program! It was not a denominationally-originated program, but it was a program nevertheless.

Yes, program-based ministries are alive and well in many churches. And they are blending beautifully with exciting new ministries.

## Premature Obituary #3: Traditional Worship Will Disappear as the Oldest Generation Dies

I have been blessed as I visited churches with exciting contemporary worship. And I have been equally blessed with the rich messages of the old hymns. I believe the church has benefitted from both styles of worship.

In recent history, worship styles have not been monolithic. In earlier eras the dichotomy was formal versus informal or liturgical versus nonliturgical. Like the church in years past, it would seem as though the church of today would welcome a variety of worship expressions.

Indeed the empirical evidence seems to support this concept. New contemporary worship services are increasing, but the traditional worship styles have not lost their significance to a large portion of the population. One recent study of attitudes toward hymns in the worship service found that only 8 percent of the adult population disliked hymns sung during a worship service. Even more fascinating was the revelation that of all type groups — unchurched, busters, boomers, singles, men, women, etc. — objection to hymns was maximum of 20 percent in any one group. [11]

The traditional worship service has a rich heritage in America. Its role does not appear to be diminishing despite the increasing number of newer models.

## Premature Obituary #4: The Sunday School Will Not Survive the 21st Century

Sunday School in America has experienced declines in both enrollment and attendance for many years. While most of this decline occurred in mainline denominations, evangelical churches have not been immune.

Because Sunday School was declining and off-campus small groups were increasing, many observers predicted that cell groups would replace the Sunday School in America. However, from 1991 to 1992, involvement in small groups (other than Sunday School) has declined over 30 percent. [12] Currently only 6 percent of adults are involved in a church-related small group. [13] Yet, Sunday School has shown signs of renewal and new visions. This topic will be discussed more fully in chapter 3.

## Premature Obituary #5: Confrontational Evangelism Is Dead

Terminology is very important here. Some use the terms confrontational evangelism and cold-call evangelism synonymously. Cold-call evangelism takes place when a person or evangelistic team attempts to share the gospel with a stranger. Confrontational evangelism is simply sharing the truth-claims of Jesus Christ so that a person must accept or reject the Savior.

Admittedly, cold-call evangelism is becoming increasingly difficult. Getting into the home of a stranger, for example, is nearly impossible in some communities. Yet there are still times when God gives us opportunities to share our faith with someone we have just met. Cold-call evangelism is more difficult today, but it is not dead.

Confrontational evangelism, on the other hand, is a biblical mandate. We cannot be Great Commission witnesses unless we confront people with the gospel. Relationship evangelism, friendship evangelism, small-group evangelism, and lifestyle evangelism are all important. But, ultimately, the unsaved person must be confronted with his or her lostness. That person must be told of the one Way of salvation. Look for a renewed emphasis on confrontational evangelism, particularly in the traditional church.

## Premature Obituary #6: We Are Living in a Post-Denominational Era

The bandwagon is loaded with pundits declaring the end of denominations. Indeed, the decline of Protestant mainline denominations since World War II is startling. Mainline Presbyterians, for example, have lost one-third of their membership since 1960, in spite of their merger. That denomination now accounts for less than 3 percent of the American population, falling from 6 percent in 1960.[14]

Experts cite the decline of mainline bodies as clear evidence that denominations are relics of a nineteenth century past. They also point to the indulged boomer generation, with their time and money greed, as further reason to believe that denominations will not survive the next century. The work of George Barna and others whose studies indicate a breakdown of denominational loyalty, appears to support their conclusions.

Although the statistical evidence is based on accurate data and well-done surveys, the information fails to discern the core reasons behind eroding denominational loyalty. The reasons are twofold.

First, many of the declining denominations have abandoned their theological heritage and identity. R. Albert Mohler, president of The Southern Baptist Theological Seminary, says the problem is primarily one of theology: "So many of these denominations have moved to the theological left and, as they have moved, they have abandoned not only their denomination's distinctives, but they have abandoned basic issues of Christian orthodoxy."[15] Denominations have lost their original focus: an institutional commitment to carry forth the doctrines of the faith and the gospel mission to the world.

A second reason behind the decline of some denominations is that the institution and its bureaucracy gained priority over the local churches. The denomination, begun initially as an entity for the churches, became a self-promoting body, forgetting that it was created to serve the local churches that carried its identity.

All too often, the person in the pew could not identify whatsoever with the proclamations and procedure of the national headquarters. Mohler suggests a "radical idea" to enable denominations to survive in the twenty-first century. He believes that the denomination itself does not have a mission. "I believe it is the local church that has the mission." He adds that one of the great tasks of this generation is "to de-institutionalize and re-congregationalize the denomination."[16] The focus must return to the local church.

Sweet also sees a potentially healthy future for denominations. "It will be a while yet before the bell tolls for denominations, if ever. Denominations may even get stronger. But denominations will find health only as heritages not as hierarchies."[17] Sweet too urges that the focus return to local churches. "They will get stronger more on a micro level than on the macro level of national systems and bureaucracies."[18]

We are not living in a post-denominational era. We are in a neo-denominational age. Some denominations will get stronger as they claim without apology the Christian truths upon which they were founded and function as true instruments of service and identity for their member churches.

Many traditional churches will be in partnership with these resurging denominations. The new denomination will provide a confessional identity for these churches, while giving assistance and resources so that the local church can carry forth the mission which is truly hers.

## When Traditional Churches Change

In *Eating the Elephant*, I wrote about instituting change in a traditional church.[19] The book you are now reading predicts a profound renewal of the traditional church in the next century. Before we proceed further, however, the issue of change should be discussed briefly.

Because some pastors and leaders of traditional churches have become convinced that their ministries are becoming ineffective, they have instituted significant changes in their churches. Sometimes these changes have done more harm than good.

The model for change that has been used in these churches was borrowed largely from the corporate world. Yet Alan L. Wilkins in his book *Developing Corporate Character*, warns that the long-standing corporate organization is hurt when change is made unwisely. He calls this process the "destruction of corporate character."[20] There is a warning here for churches.

Wilkins noted three major mistakes made by corporate leaders as change agents. First, many tried to imitate piecemeal other successful organizations. He said that "the result was typically cynicism rather than hoped-for productivity improvements."[21] Similar effects have been observed when established churches attempted to introduce aspects of other "model churches" into their unique church culture.

Second, some corporate executives attempted to add new emphases which did not mesh well with the existing corporate culture. Wilkins concludes that the hoped-for synergy between the new elements and the existing structure often is impossible. Likewise, many established church leaders fail to ask the question: How will the introduction of this new ministry, program, person, etc. affect the well-being and effectiveness of that which presently exists?

Finally, Wilkins noted, change is sometimes introduced in a revolutionary manner. Large numbers of new executives replace the "old guard." The leadership brings in new methods, structures, and hiring patterns over a short time. The old reward system is replaced by a new system. When revolution comes to a corporation, performance usually does not improve. Employees do not understand the dynamics of the changes. Instead of sharing the vision, they learn how to resist changes, sometimes while appearing to support them. Churches can also experience this backlash. Many of the members in rapidly-changing traditional churches simply leave because they neither understand nor support the leadership's vision. They are unwilling to support the church because it is no longer "their" church. The church's character has been devalued.

Though church leaders should be extremely careful when borrowing ideas from the secular world, Wilkins' offers some valuable suggestions for changing an organization without removing its character. The following are noteworthy for this discussion:[22]

- Honor the past.

- Return to the past for inspiration and instruction.

- Identify the principles that will remain constant.

- Find current examples of success.

Neither Wilkins nor I advocate a "changeless" organization or church. However, the first step toward change in an established organization is to identify what has been successful. The traditional church is being blessed by God in many ways, and that should be our starting point. I believe the traditional church may be headed toward a great renewal through many of its *existing* emphases and ministries.

### A Time to Waken the Giant

The traditional church is not dead, although, in some cases, she may need to be roused from her sleep. Because the traditional church represents such a large portion of American Christianity, her renewal could introduce a revival to our nation. A mere 1 percent net growth in these churches would result in one- to two-million people reached for Christ! Imagine the possibilities with even more growth.

This book presents trends which point to the wakening of the giant which could make an incredible impact on our nation. Rather than focusing on the problems in these churches, as some have advocated, *Giant Awakenings* shows the readers exciting developments in some long-standing traditional approaches.

Numerous scholars, sociologists, and historians have been speaking about the future of the church. The imminent arrival of a new century and a new millennium has undoubtedly engendered much of the interest. While many of their insights have been worthy contributions, most of them miss the key factor in the future of all churches.

True awakening and change in our churches is not so much a factor of sociological and demographic issues, as it is a spiritual hunger and renewal. Of all the trends I see in churches, particularly in traditional churches, this trend is the most important.

For you who have read or studied the history of revivals and awakening in America, you will notice a remarkable similarity between the historic signs of awakenings and the developments in many traditional churches. The similarities are not coincidental. I believe God is about to restore our land and turn us from our wicked ways. And I also believe that the traditional church will be a key instrument in that revival.

Look at some of the signs of historic awakenings. These signs are some of the very issues we will discuss in-depth in this book.

## A Hunger for Prayer

Awakenings can be anticipated when a nation degenerates to its lowest level. As one historian of awakenings noted: "When disobedience, immorality, secularism, and godlessness prevail, the situation is ripe for revival. This sounds much like our current situation. Probably never have we been more in need."[23]

Praying churches are multiplying across our nation, and many of these are traditional churches. People are recognizing that the only hope for our land is a humbling of ourselves in fervent prayer. Many boring, generalized prayer meetings are turning into times of deep repentance, intense intercession, and fervent prayer. Lausanne Committee traveling prayer representative Glenn Sheppard observes: "The more I go and the more places I turn, the more I see that the church that kneels to pray is the church that stands the tallest."[24] Perhaps the greatest sign of awakening in the traditional church is the renewal of fervent prayer.

## A Return to the Bible

In many traditional churches, a renewed hunger for deep, biblical teaching abounds. Superficial teaching and preaching is no longer acceptable. One church historian noted of past revivals: "Believers . . . become evangelical in thought and theology. [They] return to New Testament spirit and methods. There is a quest for the apostolic faith and way of doing things. The Bible becomes the pattern for service."[25]

## A Priority for Evangelism

Another sign of awakening in traditional churches is that priority is given to evangelism. Salvation through Christ is seen as humanity's greatest need. Winning the lost to personal faith in Christ is central. The awakening that is taking place is restoring proper priorities as redeeming love becomes the key theme.

## A Concern for the Whole Person

While evangelism should be the priority for churches, those churches that are waking up to the call of revival are no less concerned about the temporal needs of people. New social ministries are increasing as God convicts believers about the great needs of suffering humanity. Historically, the established church has been the impetus behind orphanages, hospitals, schools, and a wealth of other ministries. Many of our needs-based institutions were born in revival. It may very well happen again in the twenty-first century.

## From Passivity to Salt and Light

In recent decades many American churches have retreated into a figurative shell as the forces of secular society have grown increasingly evil. Our nation is in its worst moral condition ever, and these churches have taken a strong biblical stand. The postmodern culture has influenced the American church more than the church has influenced culture.

However, in an ever increasing number of traditional churches, that complacency is no longer evident. These churches are taking a loving but firm biblical stand that flies in the face of the prevailing worldview. They are truly becoming the salt of the earth and the light of the world.

## Mercy Drops Now, Showers of Blessing Soon

When my first son, Sam, was born, I started singing some of the great hymns to him. (I think Sam was the only person who could stand to listen to me!) By the time he was two he had chosen his favorite which he sang often: "There will be showers of blessing; showers of blessing we need. Mercy drops 'round us are falling, but for the showers we plead."

I see "mercy drops" today in our traditional churches—signs of an imminent awakening. Because these signs precede the "showers of blessing," the hard, statistical evidence is not yet apparent.

As a student of both the history of revivals and the local church, I see a significant movement in many local churches that indicates a great renewal is near. As you journey through the pages of this book, I pray that you too will see how God is beginning a great work. Above all, I pray that you will share my burden for the renewal of the traditional church, and that God will use you as an instrument of that revival. The giant has been sleeping for years. Let us now see why the giant may very well awaken to one of the greatest moves of God in our nation's history.

# Chapter One

# "If My People . . ."
# Church Trend 1:
# The Great Prayer Movement

All of our past failure, all of our past inefficiency and insufficiency, all of our past unfruitfulness in service, can be banished now, once and for all, if we only give prayer its proper place.

—An Unknown Christian

IF CHURCH FUTURISTS ARE indeed overlooking some of the spiritual aspects of the twenty-first-century church, we must discern where the most glaring omissions occur. With only a few exceptions, the pundits fail to see the immeasurable impact that prayer has upon churches.[1] In this chapter we will examine a prayer movement that may be unprecendented since the Acts revival at Pentecost (see Acts 2:40–47).

One may question if it is accurate to expect the prayer movement to impact traditional churches. Several responses to this question are in order. First, the sheer number of traditional churches means that the movement is more likely to find its way into these fellowships. If my observation that over 90 percent of American churches are traditional is correct, then more traditional churches will undoubtedly be touched by the prayer movement.

Second, members of traditional churches are hungry for a great touch of God's Spirit. They know that their churches are falling short of God's plan for them, yet they feel uncomfortable abandoning many of their distinctives to change to a nontraditional model. In their hunger, these believers often turn to God with an uncommon fervency in prayer.

Third, a phenomenon that offers no easy explanation is the presence of a singular prayer warrior in many traditional churches. One person is touched by God in an extraordinary manner. He or she (though most of the prayer warriors that I have known are females) has a burden for prayer that will not abate. Through formal prayer ministries or simply through informal channels, this person becomes a leader and a conduit through which the burden for prayer spreads to the congregation.

Finally, we must ultimately recognize that a sovereign God moves as He pleases. He is choosing to move among churches whose flame has ebbed to no more than a flicker. God is touching traditional churches because He desires for the vast majority of churches to awaken from their spiritual slumber.

## Before the Movement

In a few pages I will discuss some of the organized movements of prayer that are gaining momentum. Before these movements became organized, however, God was stirring up His leaders and future leaders individually. I believe my own story is one of thousands that can be told in varying detail. The prayer movement actually started with these individuals over the past ten to twenty years.

In 1982, I was a struggling seminary student experiencing the typical shortages of money and time. At the peak of one particularly frustrating time, my three-year-old son, Sam, began to show signs of illness. Knowing the pattern of childhood sicknesses, my wife and I showed concern, although we were not very worried.

By the next day, however, a low-grade fever had become a dangerous and climbing temperature. Physicians and other medical personnel treated Sam for two days, but he remained in grave danger. Finally, his pediatrician came to my wife and me and told us that Sam's only hope was prayer. We took her words literally and seriously.

The next evening was a Wednesday night, a time when many churches gather for corporate prayer. At the precise time that many of these churches were praying for Sam, his fever broke. He then uttered three of the most beautiful words I have ever heard, "I'm hungry, Daddy."

While Sam's healing gives glory to a sovereign and powerful God, his story is not unique among the greater Christian community. God's healing power is evident day after day around the globe.

I shared this story not so much to provide another testimony of healing prayers, as to show you how God dealt with me individually. Through this incident He sent a clear message about the critical importance of prayer in my future ministry. Prayer was to be the foundation of all ministries that somehow touched my life.

Two years later another dramatic event reinforced my earlier encounter with God. My father, also named Sam, was diagnosed with a form of rapidly-spreading cancer. I was devastated at the thought of losing my dad—my best friend. Again, I turned to prayer warriors to intercede for a physical healing.

This time God's answer was "no." Dad died within two months of his diagnosis. My prayers for a physical healing were answered with an eternal healing.

Yet, again I was impressed with God's message about prayer. He wanted prayer to be a priority in all my future ministry work. Little did I know that, in less than one month, I would become pastor of a church. Over the next decade, God led me to help traditional churches develop a new awareness of the importance of prayer. At a recent convention where several of my seminary classmates were gathered, I shared my story about God directing me to lead churches to greater depths of prayer. Amazingly, to the man, each of these pastors shared similar experiences. About ten years earlier they, too, sensed God's calling to lead churches in a new awareness of the power of prayer. Subsequently, all of them served as pastors of traditional churches. And God's hand was upon their work.

## Churches Around our Nation

Several years ago, I was asked to evaluate a church for growth opportunities. After a week or two of demographic research, interviews, and on-site examination, I made a report to the church. As a result of that initial experience, I became involved in a church consultation ministry. Although I never became a full-time church consultant, my work with local churches has allowed me to study churches and speak with church leaders across our nation.

Most of my work has been with traditional churches seeking a renewed focus and a new dream. One particular church, however, asked me to help them accommodate an already-renewed growth. They were literally running out of space for all age groups.

I studied the church statistics for the most recent five years along with the demographic data for a five-mile radius of the area. The sixty-year-old church was in a sparsely-populated, blue-collar and agricultural community. The growth rate of the community was almost zero, yet the church was experiencing rapid growth.

When I made an on-site visit, I was shocked at what I saw. The church building was in deplorable condition. The parking lot had several pieces of asphalt missing. The roof was leaking in three sections. Offices had been subdivided, with volunteer labor, to make multiple Sunday School classes. Only rough concrete remained as a floor.

How could such a worn, rag-tag church building be the home of rapid growth? I discovered the answer in my initial interviews with church members.

Three years earlier, a group of men began a daily 5:00 A.M. prayer time for the church. From that small beginning, prayer exploded in power throughout the church. Lost and unchurched people were literally drawn to the formerly staid and stale church. Like the first church in Jerusalem, this church was, "enjoying the favor of all people" (Acts 2:47).

One particularly fascinating interview I conducted was with a young couple who had recently become Christians as a result of the church's ministry. On more than one occasion, they hired a baby-sitter to keep their preschool child during worship services because the preschool department had no more room! Imagine all this to attend a traditional church!

It should be no surprise, then, that the role of prayer in the renewal and growth of the church is receiving increased attention.[2] Yet church futurists continue to focus on peripheral issues rather than the key issue of prayer.

In 1994, Billy Graham spoke to the North American Conference for Itinerant Evangelists in Louisville, Kentucky. As the famed evangelist reflected on a half-century of ministry, he paused a moment, then continued. "You know," he said, "more than any point in my ministry I am aware of the tremendous power of prayer. I really believe we are in the midst of spiritual awakening. Wouldn't it be terrible if you slept through this movement of God?"

## The Great Prayer Movement

It may seem ironic that a spiritual awakening is taking place when our nation is in its worst spiritual condition ever. But God's sovereign hand seems to move mightily when God's people are desperate about their situation. The entire book of Judges chronicles the cycle of Israel's spiritual rebellion, oppression by foreign forces, and plea for God's hand of mercy. For example, in one story the Israelites rebelled against God and served the false gods of Baal and Asherah. God's anger burned against the people, and they were subjected to foreign oppression for eight years. But, finally, God heard the cries of the Israelites, and He raised up a deliverer, Othniel (Judges 3:1–11).

Today our nation is worshiping an array of false gods: materialism, secularism, hedonism, relativism, New Age mysticism, and others. We are seeing again and again the results of our moral decay and misplaced worship: soaring crime rates, sexually-transmitted diseases, breakdown of the family, and declining educational standards. Yet God is raising up a new army of prayer warriors to fight this spiritual warfare. And many of these prayer warriors are in traditional churches across America.

The prayer movement is by no means limited to one denomination or Christian group. C. Peter Wagner observes: "The hunger for prayer knows no denominational boundaries. Evangelical, mainline, charismatic, Pentecostal, Episcopal, fundamentalist, Lutheran, Baptist, restorationist, Reformed, Mennonite, holiness, Calvinistic, dispensational, Wesleyan, or you-name-it kinds of churches are surprising themselves at the growing interest of prayer."[3]

In Southern Baptist circles, the topic of a prayer movement is receiving more than passing notice. Henry T. Blackaby, director for prayer and spiritual awakening at the Southern Baptist Home Mission Board, stated that "I am very, very convinced that God has begun a movement of revival and that we're seeing things happen . . . that we have not seen in our lifetime."[4] Avery Willis, a Southern Baptist Foreign Mission Board leader said, "I've been operating on the premise that God has already promised revival."[5] Roy Edgemon, another denominational leader, sees the sad state of our nation as the reason for many desperate prayers: "I see the agony. . . . Everywhere I go, everywhere I turn, people are hurting. . . . *We need desperately the touch of God in our land as we've never needed it in our history. This is the time for it.*"[6]

Many prayer movements across our nation are being coordinated and synchronized by the A.D. 2000 and Beyond movement. This movement strives to be a prayer catalyst for evangelism, church planting, and outreach in the world. In addition to this movement's worldwide impact, many long-standing traditional churches in America are being touched by a renewed emphasis on prayer and spiritual awakening.

## The Korean Example

As I move among the people in traditional churches, I am often asked about the churches in Korea. It seems as though God has used these churches as models and examples for their American counterparts. The prayer movement began in Korea over fifty years ago, but it only gained notice in America in the early 1970s. It received its greatest attention in 1988. Seoul hosted the Olympic games that year, so the Christians in the area decided to have a single gathering for prayer. On August 15, 1988 one million Christians gathered in an outdoor area to pray specifically for the Olympics![7]

Korean Christians now meet routinely for pre-dawn meetings. Peter Wagner, during one of his visits to Korea, was scheduled to attend one of these meetings. However, a severe storm that had taken more than sixty lives the previous night, continued to rage the next day: "The rain and wind were so ferocious at 5:00 the next morning that I wondered if anyone at all would leave their homes for a prayer meeting. But the driver showed up, we went to the church and arrived after the meeting started; if someone had not reserved seats for us, we would not have had a place to sit. The 4000-seat sanctuary was packed! What a prayer meeting!"[8]

Wagner relates another time when he attended an early-morning prayer gathering at the Myong-Song Presbyterian Church. This church had prayer meetings at 4:00 A.M., 5:00 A.M., and 6:00 A.M., with a total attendance of 12,000![9]

Many Korean churches are expanding their prayer ministries with all-night sessions. It is conceivable that 250,000 Christians in Seoul are praying every Friday night for the entire evening.

Yet other churches in Korea have purchased prayer mountains on which they have built prayer retreat centers. Hundreds and thousands of Korean Christians are always present on these mountains.

American Christians like models to emulate. For many years the model of cell groups in Korea was held high as *the* method of church growth for our nation. While cell groups may very well be a God-blessed methodology for us, I do not believe it is the key lesson we should learn from the Koreans. Our lesson is not so much the methodology or principle (cell groups), but the power behind the principle (prayer).

Fortunately, many American pastors and other Christian leaders have returned from Korea with a life-changing testimony of the power of prayer. These messages are influencing our churches immeasurably. The traditional church, particularly, has felt the impact of these testimonies. Look for a renewal of the traditional church that has as its foundation a fervent, lives-changing, prayer ministry. The dynamic church of the twenty-first century will be first a house of prayer.

## Historical Evidence of Prayer Awakenings

Historically, the most significant trends in the church are prefaced by extraordinary prayer. Wise futurists will look to the lessons of history to see the shape of the twenty-first century church. A few noteworthy examples will provide a glimpse into the relationship of the church and prayer.

### The Jerusalem Church

The very first church provides a clear example of the centrality of prayer to effect new directions for the church. While most discussion centers around the explosive power of the Holy Spirit on the day of Pentecost (Acts 2:1-47), Jesus gave His followers important instructions *prior* to this day. He told them to "wait for the gift my Father promised, which you have heard me speak about" (Acts 1:4).

The response of His followers to this mandate to wait was to gather for intensive prayer. "They all joined together constantly in prayer, along with the women and Mary the mother of Jesus, and with his brothers" (Acts 1:14). Before the first, true church awakening took place, prayer was evident among the people.

The coming of the Holy Spirit at Pentecost was a powerful event. It initiated the age of the New Testament church. While certain developments were unique to that moment, some unchanging principles still apply to the church today. One is the principle of prayer. The first church was among a plethora of churches over the centuries renewed by God through prayer.

### Awakenings during the Eighteenth and Nineteenth Centuries

The pattern of awakenings in the church during the eighteenth and nineteenth centuries was similar to the cycle of sin, judgment, and renewal Israel experienced in the book of Judges. The eighteenth century included the European and Revolutionary wars and the revival of deism, transcendentalism, and Unitarianism, while the nineteenth century was an era of slavery controversy, liberalism, and evolutionism.[10]

After each era of social and moral decline, a new era of church awakening was ushered in by God. The First Great Awakening reversed the course of both sacred and secular history in America, Germany, and Britain. Instruments of God in this revival included some of history's greatest preachers: James Davenport, Jonathan Edwards, Gilbert Tennent, John Rowland, George Whitefield, and Shubal Stearns. While social history records great progress in education, politics, medicine, and other humanitarian endeavors, church history records a return to the basics, traditions if you will. Lewis Drummond notes that in the First Great Awakening the church returned to "apostolic simplicity."[11]

The late eighteenth and early nineteenth centuries were the years of the Second Great Awakening. While the First Awakening began with the New England Congregationalists and Presbyterians, the Second Awakening first involved Methodists and Baptists. Once again the church was profoundly affected by the great surge of revival power. And yet again, God returned the church to the basics of the Christian faith through the instruments of praying men and women. Two North Carolina Presbyterian ministers, James McGready and Barton Stone, were such instruments, primarily because of their fervency in prayer.

Numerous other accounts of church renewal preceded by prayer could be noted: the Cane Ridge Revival, the Great Nineteenth-Century Awakening with Charles G. Finney and D. L. Moody, and the Lay Prayer Revival of an overlapping era. Through these and other movements, the church was impacted greatly. What were some of the results of these revivals in the church?

### Worldwide Awakenings in the Church

Church historian Earle E. Cairns notes with profound simplicity that "prayer ranks first in the coming of revival."[12] In his study of prayer and revivals from 1726 to the present, Cairns notes that each renewal began with organized prayer groups. "Prayer preceded the Scottish revival of 1742 and 1839. Moody, Chapman, and other nineteenth-century persons had many organized prayer groups praying for their work. Mrs. Warren organized thousands to pray for the Torrey meetings of Australia and then for his meetings in Britain. Indeed, Torrey's call to lead in worldwide revival came in a prayer meeting at Moody Bible Institute. *There cannot be revival unless Christians pray for it.*"(emphasis added)[13]

At risk of redundancy, I will again say that one of the profound results of these prayer awakenings was a return to the more traditional elements of the church: expository preaching, organized Bible study, a new zeal for evangelism, and an affirmation of orthodoxy. Certainly the church changed some of its methodologies, but it reaffirmed the elements of the faith that have their roots in centuries past.

We have thus affirmed that prayer is the key element in the historic awakenings of the church, and that the traditional church is touched significantly by these awakenings. We have further seen that the modern church is in the midst of a great prayer movement. We will now look at specific ways that the prayer movement is manifesting itself in individual churches across our land.

## Signs of Prayer in the Local Church

Pastor Mark Hearn is a friend who was also a fellow seminary student of mine. Of the many seminary students I knew, I considered Mark a leader among leaders. He has a history of successful, growing pastorates.

A few years ago, Mark became pastor of Grace Baptist Church located in a downtown transition area of Evansville, Indiana. Steeped in traditions and with little demographic growth in its location, the church was a classic case of the old, dying, downtown church.

Pastor Hearn struggled with the direction of the church. Should they relocate? Should they start a satellite church? Should they focus the church's ministry primarily to the inner city? Because so many major decisions were on the horizon, he realized that only God could provide the answers, resources, and strength he needed. Though Pastor Hearn already knew prayer was essential to the Christian, the moment of need at Grace Baptist Church made him desire more than ever a touch of God's power. He turned to prayer.

Under his leadership, the church began various prayer ministries that became a vital part of the very life of the church. Within weeks prayers, articulated and written, began to be answered. A new sense of expectancy enveloped the church. On one occasion, a leader in the prayer ministry decided to gather a list of recently-answered prayers. To the surprise of many, the single-spaced list covered twenty pages!

Today, Grace Baptist Church sees people accept Christ as their Lord and Savior almost every week. Virtually every one of those saved were people who had been concerns of prayer for weeks and months.

Major decisions still await Pastor Hearn and Grace Baptist Church. But now the people move forward in confidence that the future is in God's hands, not their own. Their traditional church has indeed been renewed by the power of prayer.

### The Statistical Evidence.

In earlier works on church growth, I cited prayer as the foundational growth principle.[14] I also stated that prayer is a mandate for the church and the individual believer regardless of numerical growth results. Yet I wondered if a statistical relationship existed between prayer and numerical growth.

In 1991, C. Kirk Hadaway published a book that has become an invaluable resource for church growth enthusiasts. Hadaway statistically tested several church growth "principles" such as evangelistic outreach, Sunday School enrollment, exciting worship, pastoral leadership, and others. Hadaway categorized the churches he studied into different groups, among them "plateaued" and "breakout" churches. A plateaued church is one that has experienced modest decline or growth for several years but, essentially, has changed little in numerical size. A breakout church was formerly a plateaued church, but is now experiencing significant growth.

The results of Hadaway's study were amazing. He found that "*71 percent* of breakout churches report an increased emphasis on prayer over the past several years as compared to only 40 percent of churches which continued on the plateau."[15] Hadaway views the statistical difference as significant. "This rather large difference indicates that one part of the revitalization which has taken place in breakout churches came in the form of a *renewed emphasis on prayer.*"[16]

It is also important to note that the 71 percent figure may understate the role of prayer for growth. The churches represented by that number reported an *increased* emphasis on prayer. Other growing churches may have already reported strong prayer ministries.

### Prayer Shields

Another important manifestation of the prayer movement in local churches is the increasing number of pastors and other Christian leaders who are seeking prayer intercessors. A prayer

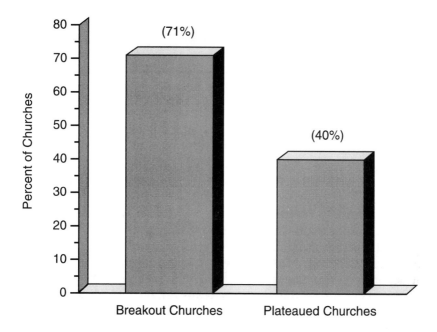

**Figure 1.1: Churches Reporting an Increased Emphasis on Prayer**

Source: C. Kirk Hadaway, *Church Growth Principles: Separating Fact from Fiction* (Nashville: Broadman, 1991)

intercessor, after seeking God's permission to do so, commits a portion of his or her day to pray for a specific person. Day after day, the intercessor brings prayer needs for the person to the throne of God. Several intercessors may pray for the same person daily. The power of prayer that emmanates from their intercession becomes a "prayer shield" around the Christian leader.[17]

Such an unusual and extraordinary manifestation of prayer is fast becoming the norm in traditional churches across our land. Rarely a week passes that a pastor or other Christian leader does not share with me testimonies about their prayer shield. They share some truly miraculous stories of God's intervention.

But more important than the specific interventions is the ongoing empowerment by God for these leaders. One pastor recently told me about the almost unbelievable change in his life and ministry after a prayer shield began to cover him daily. His sermon preparation time became exciting and enlightening. God gave him insights into Scripture that he had never known in twenty years of ministry. The sermons themselves became instruments to change lives Sunday after Sunday. And the pastor, who had always been weak in personal evangelism, began to lead people to Christ regularly.

The old rural church he pastored responded to their newly-empowered leader. Slowly attendance declines reversed. For the first time in three decades, the church experienced an increase in worship attendance!

The changes, however, were not limited to statistics and numbers. New ministries were begun. Mission projects and mission giving increased tenfold. And, much to the amazement of the church members, two feuding families were reconciled to one another after almost eight years of strife!

This traditional, rural church had no demographic reason for its turnaround. Its experience defied church growth "laws." Yet the last time I heard, the church was still growing and reaching out to its community in unprecedented fashion.

Scant attention has been given to the prayer shield phenomenon by observers and church futurists. However, this very exciting aspect of prayer may be one of the keys to the renewal of the traditional church in the twenty-first century.

### Prayer Outside the Walls

C. Peter Wagner identifies another fascinating aspect of prayer in the local church. "In the decade of the 1990s, God has been surfacing a concept, which, at least for me, is invigoratingly new. A few have been practicing it for a while, but now God is showing the whole Body of Christ how to pray *in* the community."[18] Churches across America are not only praying within the walls of their church buildings, they are discovering exciting and innovative ways to pray outside the walls.

One method of praying outside the walls is prayerwalks. Steve Hawthorne defines prayerwalking as "praying on site with insight." Hawthorne comments, "This is intercessory prayer . . . praying in the very place in which you expect your prayers to be answered."[19] The idea of prayerwalking is to pray with your actions as well as your words and thoughts.

The best revival meeting in which I participated took place in a medium-sized traditional church in south Alabama. On the second day of the revival, the pastor asked me to pray with him as we walked outside the church into the community. A few of the church leaders joined us as we prayed for the church to be a mighty instrument of evangelism and ministry in the community.

That prayerwalk was one of the most moving experiences of my life. God honored the faithfulness of His servants, and a *real* revival came to the church.

Another example of praying outside the walls includes praise marches, where churches come together to pray for their city. On May 23, 1992, 200 praise marches took place in as many cities. Forty of the praise marches were in Europe and 160 in the United States and Canada; more than 600,000 people participated. In Austin, Texas, for example, at least 20,000 walked in praise. Specific prayers were lifted up for the city and a large offering was received and given to the city of Austin for the Children's Hospital.[20]

## Prayers for Corporate Repentance and Unity

In their book Setting Your Church Free, Neil T. Anderson and Charles Mylander describe in detail another significant prayer movement in local churches. The authors believe that the lack of evangelistic and spiritual growth in many churches is the result of corporate bondage. They define corporate bondage as "unresolved personal and spiritual issues that inhibit churches from being the most God wants them to be—free in Christ."[21]

Many churches, according to Anderson and Mylander have corporately renounced the sins that have prevented the church body from being a dynamic testimony for the Savior. These services of corporate repentance and prayers for unity are taking place in an ever increasing number of churches. Just look at some examples of renouncing and confession taken from various actual churches, using their own words.

- We renounce complacency and contentment.

- We renounce a critical and judgmental spirit.

- We renounce gossip and pettiness.

- We renounce our distrust of God's chosen and faithful leaders.

- We renounce our poor stewardship of time, talent, and treasures.

- We renounce lukewarmness and weariness in doing the Lord's work.

- We renounce our self-focus that produces apathy to the lost.

- We renounce attacks on leadership.

- We renounce the spirit of fear that paralyzes open sharing, involvement, service, and evangelism.

- We renounce any footholds gained by the evil one through past hurts and traumas.

- We renounce Satan's use of discouragement as a tool against us.[22]

Again, this aspect of the prayer movement has hardly been noticed by those who look for trends in the church. And again, it is the traditional church that has been most affected by the prayers for corporate repentance and unity. The traditional church typically has a lengthy history, some of which is healthy, some of which is unhealthy. It is that unhealthy aspect of its past that churches are bringing before God. The Lord is hearing the prayers and answering with renewal and revival. It is a movement that will grow into the next century.

### Reclaiming the Tradition through Prayer

In this chapter I have shared but a small part of the great prayer movement that is moving our churches, particularly traditional churches, to a new great awakening. The Christian world has barely noticed; and all but a few in the secular world are oblivious to the movement. I suppose many slept through earlier awakenings; many will do so again. But those who have ears, listen: prayer is changing our churches and our land!

New methodologies, contemporary worship services, cell groups — all are instruments God has used and may continue to use in the years ahead. But they are only methodologies. Something far deeper and more significant is taking place today.

Leonard Sweet notes that in "the deterministic world of modern science, prayer didn't make sense."[23] However, he continues, "The postmodern world, where ultimate reality is spirit, has virtually returned us to a more biblical outlook on the world."[24] Citing Ken Briggs of the *New York Times Magazine*, Sweet notes, "*A prayer revival is the most powerful, least documented development within modern American religion today*."[25] Briggs is one of the few voices of understanding in a wilderness of spiritual misunderstanding.

According to Sweet, the "new paradigm churches" will reclaim the tradition of prayer. In reality, the new paradigm churches are a return to an old paradigm, i.e. traditional churches. Consider

Sweet's plea for a return to the basics: "It is time for some hermeneutical retrievals of the old-fashioned 'prayer meeting,' the 'concerts of prayer,' and 'prayer breakfasts.' It is also important to celebrate 'answered prayers' publicly, something already being called by some as 'thank you notes to God.'"[26]

King Solomon led ancient Israel in the building of a new and magnificent temple to be the home for the presence of God. Great times of celebration, sacrifice, and consecration marked the completion of the temple. Crowds gathered for celebration from all parts of Israel.

Finally the celebration ended. The people returned to their homes and Solomon returned to the royal palace. That very night the Lord appeared to King Solomon and told him what really mattered. Temples and palaces were okay, but a people turned to God in prayer was the sacrifice of service God required. The Lord spoke these words to the king: "If my people, who are called by my name, will humble themselves and pray and seek my face and turn from their wicked ways, then will I hear from heaven and will forgive their sin and will heal their land" (2 Chron. 7:14).

God's people *are* praying. Traditional churches are being renewed. The prayer movement is sweeping America.

Over the past several years I have accumulated many books and articles about possible spiritual awakenings in America. Most of them predict that an awakening is *near*. It is my belief, however, that the abundant evidence of a great prayer movement means that the awakening is *now*. Many traditional churches are being renewed. Look for even more fruit-bearing among these churches in the twenty-first century. And keep alert and awake. You could miss one of God's greatest moments in our land.

# Chapter 2

# "Preach the Word . . ."
# Church Trend 2: The Rediscovery of the Bible and Theology

How can a church know when it is losing significant contact with the wider society and is failing in its attempts at an effective mission in the world? . . . When it minimizes biblical truth or conduct in favor of respectability and broadmindedness.

—Bruce Shelley and Marshall Shelley

PERHAPS AN EPISODE FROM the long-running sitcom "Cheers" is not the best place to begin a discussion about the Bible. But, then again, this story depicts the strange relationship many Americans have with the Bible.

Our dubious hero, Sam the bartender, has undergone a moral transformation, at least he attempts to do so. He has made a new commitment to God (though his theology is radically askew) to live a celibate life from this day forward (Sam rarely had *one* celibate day to this point).

His commitment is strong, at least for a few hours, until an old girlfriend shows up in the bar with an explicit invitation for our amorous friend. This time the temptation is too great. Sam departs with her.

The scene of the next day has the "Cheers" friends inquiring about Sam's fall. Much to their amazement, Sam declares that "nothing happened." He tells them about his "spiritual" experience at the first motel. Prior to the would-be tryst, he opened a drawer in the bedside table. There, before his shock-widened eyes, was a Bible.

Nonetheless, he let lust overcome conviction, and tried a second motel only to have the same experience. Five motels later he gave up and went home.

Sam's friends did not have the heart to tell him about Gideon Bibles in motels. They let him believe that God was miraculously holding him to his promise through a series of divinely-placed Scriptures. The Bibles were there all along, but Sam had never seen them.

Such has been the plight of American Christianity in the past few decades. We have the Bibles, but we never see them. Almost every home in our nation has one or more Bibles, but our citizens are biblically illiterate. Only six in ten Americans know who preached the Sermon on the Mount![1] And only 52 percent identify the book of Thomas as a noncanonical book.[2]

While former communist nations hunger for scarce Bibles, Americans let their Scriptures adorn coffee tables. Walk through the Bible ministries and the Gideons report tremendous success leading seminars in Russian *public schools*. But American public schools are prohibited by the courts from even posting the Ten Commandments.

However, a new trend is taking shape. A renewed hunger for God's Word is evident in many churches. The centrality of the Bible is a tradition which is being reaffirmed across our land. This return to the Bible, one of the key marks of an awakening, is particularly notable in the traditional church.

## The Bible, Theology, and Awakenings

Lewis Drummond notes six theological signs of revival.[3] First, the church returns to the basic truths of Scripture. Complex and obscure theology is pushed aside for the fundamentals of the faith.

Similarly, the church hungers for the methodology and results of the early church. The book of Acts in particular is seen as a pattern for service and evangelistic possibilities.

Third, the message of the cross becomes central in preaching and teaching. A renewed understanding of the meaning of Christ's sacrifice overcomes complacency among the people.

Fourth, evangelism becomes the church's priority. The salvation offered by Christ is seen as humanity's greatest need. Other ministries, though vitally important, are secondary to witnessing, outreach, and evangelism.

Liberal theology dies in awakenings. Because God's work becomes so very evident to the people, anti-supernatural theology is rejected. The God of miracles is the God of the Bible. Any other view of God, any theology beyond orthodoxy, will not be affirmed.

Finally, cold orthodoxy is rejected as well. "Nothing is much 'deader' than a dead, cold, rationalistic fundamentalism. But when revival comes, though the actual theological position of conservatives may not substantially change, it suddenly comes alive and glows. That change is as needed as an overhauling of so-called liberal theology."[4]

Without exception awakenings are movements anchored in the Bible. Leaders and participants in awakenings are men and women of the Bible. "They took it as a fully inspired revelation from God, written by men who were inspired by the Holy Spirit,"[5] says church historian Earle E. Cairns of awakening leaders. He further notes, "To them the Bible was a 'self-contained and self-interpreting revelation' given by God. It was a complete, final, and binding authority on the church."[6]

In the midst of awakenings and revivals, the sovereignty of God is declared. God is seen in His holiness and justice. And the people of awakenings see themselves as depraved humanity, guilty of original and actual sin, sinners both by birth and choice.

God's provision for the forgiveness of sins through Christ's death on the cross is thus seen as an act of totally undeserved mercy. Grace takes on new meaning, and the love of God through Christ is considered the greatest gift that one person could ever receive. Preaching is needs-based in the sense that humanity's greatest need is proclaimed: a personal relationship with a forgiving and living Savior.

Much of today's writings about the church, discusses the vital necessity to meet needs. In no way would I disagree with this assessment. When Joe Boomer or Jill Buster know little other than the fact that their lives are empty, we must address those needs. The recognition and meeting of such needs is a major contribution of the nontraditional church today. Yet a church experiencing true renewal will witness an Acts-like revival where the unchurched and unbelieving world will be drawn to the church asking one essential "needs" question: "What must I do to be saved?" (Acts 16:30).

## A Seeker Movement in the Traditional Church

A theology of the unchurched has largely been the emphasis of nontraditional churches in past decades. This new emphasis, called "the seeker-church movement," is led by such nontraditional churches as Willow Creek Community Church and Saddleback Valley Community Church. Bill Hybels, senior pastor of Willow Creek, defines the seeker movement as "nothing more than a growing awareness among thousands of church leaders that local churches lost their evangelistic effectiveness many decades ago and that something should be done about it."[7]

Unfortunately this theology of the unchurched has been perceived as an "us-them" divide, causing debate and even conflict in American churches. Some traditional church leaders and churchgoers have become suspicious of anything that takes place in the innovative churches. And some nontraditional church leaders have written off any hope for traditional churches. One vocal critic of the traditional church, comparing the traditional church to the dinosaur, writes: "Both have great heritages. Both require enormous amounts of food. Both influenced their world tremendously. And both became endangered species . . . Like the dinosaur, their necks are too stiff or their eyes too nearsighted. Clearly, God doesn't care if these congregations survive."[8]

Equally acrimonious comments flow from some traditional church leaders toward the seeker-church movement or nontraditional churches. One well-known critic writes: "The obvious fallout of this preoccupation with the unchurched is a corresponding deemphasis on those who are the true church. The spiritual needs of believers are often neglected to the hurt of the body."[9]

Christians need to be aware and concerned about this divide in the body. Criticisms both ways can be healthy because corrections and adjustments need to be made. But much of the debate falls outside the biblical boundaries of speaking in love (1 Cor. 13:1).

In reality the new awareness and desire to evangelize the lost and unchurched is not the creation of either traditional or nontraditional churches per se. Rather, it is the result of an almost century-long movement to recover the authority of Scripture and live the mandates of God's Word. From that rediscovery of the Bible and theology flows a new hunger for evangelism and discipleship.

### The Rediscovery of the Bible in the Twentieth Century

Perhaps historians will mark the twentieth century as equally noteworthy to church history as the sixteenth century. The Protestant Reformation, led by such historical giants as Luther, Zwingli, and Calvin, "laid stress, not upon innovation, but upon return to primitive excellence."[10] This primitive excellence was nothing more than a rediscovery of the Bible.

As the Bible became central once again in the sixteenth century, doubts were raised about salvation by works, the validity of papal claims to supremacy, transubstantiation, clerical celibacy, and abuses in the church at Rome. The shape of history, both secular and church, was changed forever.

The twentieth-century "reformation" will also leave an indelible mark on church history. The rediscovery of the Bible and theology is touching all churches, but our focus will ultimately be upon traditional churches. We can see the rediscovery of the authority of Scripture in three distinct but overlapping movements.

### The Fundamentalist/Modernist Controversy

Early in the twentieth century, a movement developed in reaction against biblical criticism that diminished the authority of Scripture and against the growing influence of evolutionary theories. Some historians trace the movement's origins to a series of Bible Conferences of Conservative Protestants in the late nineteenth century.

Out of a conference held at Niagra in 1895, a statement of belief was issued that later became known as "the five points of fundamentalism." Those five points were the verbal inspiration of Scripture; the divinity of Jesus Christ; the virgin birth of Christ; the substitutionary atonement by Christ; and the physical resurrection and bodily return of Christ.

The term *fundamentalism* has its origins in a series of twelve tracts entitled *The Fundamentals*, with the first tract published in 1909. They were written by well-known evangelical leaders and widely distributed in America and beyond.

As an outgrowth of this movement, the World's Christian Fundamental Association was founded. Local groups and regional rallies surfaced. Eventually, nearly all Protestant churches in America became identified as either fundamentalist or modernist.

Perhaps the greatest public attention given to the movement took place in 1925 when William Jennings Bryan, the American Democratic leader, took the leadership role in the prosecution of J. T. Scopes, a school teacher in Dayton, Tennessee. Scopes was convicted of violating a state law which prohibited the teaching of biological evolution. Fundamentalists and modernists were predictably outspoken and divided over this controversy.

From the fundamentalists' point of view, their beliefs were at the very core of the gospel. Any compromise in these essentials could ultimately lead down the slippery slope toward compromise and agnosticism.

The modernists, primarily liberal Protestants, insisted that Christianity should embrace scientific discovery and biblical criticism. They attempted to form a positive synthesis between the two belief systems of science and the Bible. They viewed the fundamentalists as narrow-minded and reactionary.

Unfortunately, some of the caricatures were at least partially true. During the decade after the Scopes trial, the fundamentalist movement retreated from mainstream society. Some of the leaders became militant separatists, suspicious of anything new or innovative. Others disparaged *all* institutions of higher education, because *some* of those schools propagated higher criticism and the theory of evolution.

Furthermore, some fundamentalists overreacted to the teaching of the social implications of the gospel in liberal circles. Certainly, these liberal churches and schools were straying from orthodoxy in their failure to communicate a conversionist gospel. But the fundamentalists were wrong in rejecting the appropriateness of social ministries, justice, and equality.

The positive contributions of fundamentalism centered around its fierce allegiance to the authority of Scripture. Although some still view fundamentalism as synonymous with narrow-mindedness and anti-intellectualism, we must not forget that the true legacy of the movement was its articulate theological response to liberalism and its plea for the return of biblical basics. That legacy will be felt in the renewal of the traditional church in the twenty-first century.

## Inerrancy and the Rise of Evangelicalism

Reacting against some of the possible extrabiblical values of fundamentalism, some conservative Christians returned to a theological position now known as evangelicalism. How is the evangelical position different from fundamentalism? Perhaps the viewpoint of Billy Graham demonstrates the similarities and differences.

Like the fundamentalists, the famed evangelist consistently spoke about the need to maintain a high view of Scripture that includes a passion for evangelism. A proper theology will result in a proper soteriology, or view of salvation. And a proper soteriology will result in sincere evangelistic zeal.

But unlike the fundamentalists, Graham saw the need for advanced education that was academically on par with secular institutions. Evangelicals across America caught that vision. After World

War II, a flow of evangelical literature began to defend the gospel with intellectual vigor. That flow became a tidal wave by the early seventies.

In 1947, Fuller Theological Seminary was founded to provide quality graduate education from a clearly evangelical perspective. Several parachurch organizations were started in response to the lack of evangelistic zeal in mainline denominations. And, in 1956, the magazine *Christianity Today* was founded as an instrument for communicating critical issues of the evangelical faith.

Evangelicalism has become so widespread that fundamentalism is now often viewed as part of the larger movement. Ron Nash sees three "subcultures" in evangelicalism. "Typically three evangelical subcultures are distinguished: fundamentalism, Pentecostalism, and what, for want of a better term, can be called the evangelical mainstream."[11]

Though the three groups have differences in their belief systems, Nash emphasizes that it is the belief in the essential tenets of the faith that bind all evangelicals. "For now, it is enough to point out that fundamentalists, evangelicals, and most charismatics share a common commitment to an essential core of beliefs that include the deity of Christ, the virgin birth, the incarnation, the substitutionary atonement, the bodily resurrection of Christ, and Christ's literal return to earth at the end of the age." Concerning the three groups' view of the Bible, Nash says that "fundamentalists, evangelicals, and most charismatics share a high view of Scripture; they believe that the Bible is the Word of God and is normative for Christian belief and practice."[12]

That view of Scripture, observes Nash, is the distinguishing characteristic of evangelicals. The groups "deplore the theological fuzziness that seems to prevail in many of America's mainline churches and their education institutions."[13]

Further, "mainstream evangelicals, fundamentalists and evangelical charismatics differ from religious liberalism in their persuasion that doctrine is an essential ingredient of the Christian faith. Men and women gain God's new life by believing the gospel. Evangelicals disagree with theological liberals who often appear to suggest that the context of a person's belief is irrelevant or unimportant to his or her relationship to God."[14]

Ironically, the common bind that holds evangelicals together has also been the point of greatest debate. Harold Lindsell, who was then serving as editor of Christianity Today, wrote an explosive book, *The Battle for the Bible*,[15] in 1976. The key theme of Lindsell's book was that numbers of professed evangelicals, many of whom were in positions of prominence, had abandoned the evangelical view of Scripture.

Lindsell claimed that these individuals did not profess an inerrant view of the Bible. Inerrancy, in its simplest form, holds that the Bible is completely truthful. Lindsell maintained that this understanding of Scripture was no longer held at Fuller Theological Seminary where he had taught or among the leadership of his own denomination, the Southern Baptist Convention.

Inerrancy became such a vocal issue among evangelicals that different definitions of the doctrine were espoused. In order to bring some uniformity of understanding, over three hundred scholars gathered in Chicago in 1978 to discuss this issue. Their written statement was called "The Chicago Statement of Inerrancy." It affirmed the complete truthfulness of Scripture: "Being wholly and verbally God-given, Scripture is without error or fault in all its teaching, no less in what it states about God's act in creation, about the events of world history, and about its own literacy origins under God, than in its witness to God's saving grace in individual lives."[16]

The statement identified two major tenets of innerancy. First, the Bible is true in all that it teaches. Second, the Bible is true when it speaks on non-doctrinal subjects such as history, geography, or science. In essence, the Chicago statement rejected the view called "limited inerrancy." The Bible is not just true in some areas; it is true in all areas.

Inerrantists were criticized for having their heads in the sand about alleged discrepancies in Scripture. Some were accused of practicing bibliolatry, the worship of the Bible. Still other critics charged that inerrantists were anti-science and intellectually feeble.

Have the defenders of inerrancy adequately addressed all the challenges put forth by the critics? Is inerrancy a valid presuppositional understanding about the nature of Scripture? Though some issues remain unresolved, an objective observer must conclude that evangelical inerrantists have done well in answering the critics. Evangelical statesman Carl F. H. Henry admits that all the problems are not yet resolved, but the past responses provide grounds for optimism for the future.[17]

Whether one views evangelicalism as a continuation of the fundamentalist movement or a new movement altogether, similarities exist between the two. Both movements sought to recover a view of Scripture that they believed was consistent with historic Christianity.

And both insisted that such a view of the Bible was a requisite for true missionary and evangelistic zeal.

On the surface it would seem that evangelicals had a more cooperative spirit toward critics than fundamentalists did. Yet the inerrancy debate fueled intense, if not acrimonious, emotions.

Nonetheless a major contribution of the evangelical movement has been its focus on the authority of Scripture. This legacy is playing a role in the rediscovery of the Bible in the traditional church today.

## The Church Growth Movement

Before we return specifically to the subject of the Bible in the traditional church, one more brief historical excursion is necessary. The Church Growth Movement began when one man became concerned about anemic evangelistic results on the mission field.[18] Donald A. McGavran, a thorough-going evangelical, served as a missionary to India for the United Christian Missionary Society. After twelve years of missionary service, McGavran began to inquire into the growth of churches. He studied 145 mission stations in India and found that only eleven were keeping pace with the general population. However, nine stations had doubled in just three years, mostly through adult conversions. He asked again and again: "How do you account for growth and non-growth in identical situations where, presumably, missionaries have been equally faithful?"[19]

McGavran felt that correct theological beliefs alone were insufficient for Christian faithfulness. An evangelical view of Scripture must accompany evangelistic methodologies that reach the culture. He insisted on theological and methodological zeal. In other words, orthopraxy cannot be divorced from orthodoxy.

This conviction is crucial in our understanding of the Church Growth Movement's influence upon traditional churches today. In many of these churches the theological beliefs have not changed. The Bible is still God's Word, and an orthodox theology is still important. Nevertheless, some of these churches are lifeless and unenthusiastic about outreach. The Church Growth Movement's insistence that right theology be coupled with right practice of ministry has been an important element in the rediscovery of the Bible in traditional churches.

In the early seventies a new leader for the movement—now located at Fuller Theological Seminary—emerged. C. Peter Wagner, a devoted student and later colleague of McGavran, began applying some of McGavran's principles to local churches in America. Wagner's books became the leading sellers among church growth books in America.[20] Though critics were many, Wagner and the Church Growth Movement influenced churches across the nation significantly.

Interestingly, Wagner emphasized the absolute necessity of *both* proper theology and proper methodology. While recognizing that his books were largely methodological in their content, theological foundations, he insisted, were critical.

The Church Growth Movement's theological foundation, said Wagner, was evangelical. The purpose of the movement was not to articulate a new theology, but to ascertain how that theology could best be practiced and lived. "Dynamic movements directly involved in Christian ministry rarely begin with theological formulations," Wagner stated. "They usually begin with activists who simply assume a set of theological premises and go to work to change the world. Systematized theological work usually is developed from a movement, not vice versa."[21]

The significant contribution of the Church Growth Movement to the traditional church can best be expressed by the biblical mandate: "Do not merely listen to the word, and so deceive yourselves. Do what it says" (James 1:22). The first and second generation church growth leaders saw lack of evangelistic fruit in churches around the world. Theology was not a problem, but application was absent. In response, the Church Growth Movement advocated a plethora of methodologies in order to be faithful to Scripture and the mandate to "make disciples of all nations" (Matt. 28:19).

Unfortunately, some church leaders heard the movement's plea for application and methodology but failed to see the theological moorings to which the methodologies were anchored. As a consequence these churches implemented programs, marketing plans, and new preaching styles without considering the theological foundation for their practices. They became completely "user-friendly" but "biblically-silent" in their efforts to engender growth. One church, admittedly an extreme example, made a conscious decision to refrain from mentioning sin in its preaching and teaching, lest it offend the unredeemed the church was trying to reach.

## The Giant Awakens to Theology

Our historical excursion was necessary in order that we might more fully understand the role of theology in the traditional church today and into the future. Prior to the sixteenth century, the average Christian was virtually biblically illiterate. Because few had access to God's Word, they depended upon human mediators and interpreters. The Reformation finally broke the chains binding the Bible to the pulpit.

From the late eighteenth century to the mid-twentieth century, so-called scholars led an attack on the veracity of Scripture in the name of "intellectualism." The movements cited in this chapter were critical in awakening the church to the full truthfulness and authority of the Bible.

Partly because of the influence of the Church Growth Movement, the late twentieth-century church has made noble attempts to obey, in deeds, the mandates of Scripture. New methodologies have abounded. In many of these churches, however, the movement's plea to wed theology *and* practice was not heard. The church at the end of this century is largely deficient in its knowledge of the Bible.

One of the great signs of awakening in the church as we move toward a new century is a renewed hunger for biblical teaching and preaching. In the truest sense of the word, this direction is a move back to *traditions*. As in all past awakenings, a return to orthodox theology is becoming the norm in many churches.

While church trend watchers have made observant comments about many developments in the late twentieth century, they have largely missed this trend toward the recovery of the Bible and theology. How can we explain this significant omission?

First, many observers have failed to see the real significance behind the biblical controversies of the twentieth century. The fundamentalist/modernist controversy, the inerrancy debate, and the user-friendly church debate have all had elements of heated controversy. Not surprisingly, the controversy and disagreements received the focus of attention rather than the key issues of biblical authority and application. The controversies masked a significant movement toward rediscovery of the Bible. God's sovereign hand has been steadily moving churches toward a sound theology.

Second, the trend watchers have failed to see the enormous influence of culture upon the church. When many within the evangelical church began "doing" ministry, some did so apart from a theological foundation of truth. Many churches, therefore, tried new methodologies and techniques with little or no biblical foundations; modernity itself became the new standard for shifting sands of "truth." Culture was leading the church rather than the church obeying God's command to be salt and light in culture (Matt. 5:13–16).

Os Guinness provides a more balanced assessment when he advocates only the careful, critical use of methodologies under the watchful eye of biblical theology. "We should remember Peter Berger's contemporary warning: 'He who sups with the devil of modernity had better have a long spoon.' By all means dine freely at the table of modernity, but in God's name keep your spoon long."[22]

Guinness further relates the use of the tools of modernity to the biblical narrative of the golden calf. "We should also remember Origen's ancient principle," he says. "Christians are free to plunder the Egyptians, but forbidden to set up a golden calf. By all means plunder freely of the treasures of modernity, but in God's name make sure that what comes out of the fire that will test our life's endeavors is gold fit for the temple of God and not a late twentieth-century image of a golden calf."[23]

Though Guinness incorrectly identifies the "idolater" (he equates user-friendly megachurches with the Church Growth Movement started by McGavran), his point is well made. Methodology ("the treasures of modernity") of the late twentieth century benefits churches and God's glory only if it is anchored to the rock of biblical theology.

## The Shape of the Rediscovery of Theology in the Church

We then have several developments in modern-day evangelicalism that point toward a profound rediscovery of theology in the church. Though some say these movements cannot co-exist they actually support and balance each other. Without these developments, the church would be headed toward the extremes of cold orthodoxy on the one hand, or theologically-empty methodologies on the other.

### The Recovery Theologians

An entire new generation of evangelical theologians is calling the church to return to its theological heritage. Although some leaders are spending an inordinate amount of time criticizing contemporary churches, most are making valuable contributions that influence the local traditional church level.

For example, Thomas C. Oden, professor of theology at Drew University, offers positive advice to help churches recover the theological heritage from which many have departed. "To do this," he says, "we must return again to the careful study and respectful following of the central tradition of classical Christian interpretation of Scripture texts. This will plant us once again in our foundation so we will not sway with the stiff winds of modernity."[24]

Oden offers a proposal to "rediscover this lost treasure." First, the Christian must simply listen to the Scripture text itself. Modern interpretations abound, but the believer's first obedience is to the text rather than the generation's "new" ideas.[25]

Similarly, says Oden, the church must "reacquaint ourselves with the classical Christian writers of our faith."[26] He suggests the late seventeenth century as a reliable dividing line for listening to writers in the Christian tradition who have not been corrupted by modernity.

When seeking the wisdom of earlier church writers, Oden admits, the church will meet resistance from culture. "Now, modernity has turned that around and said the opposite: If anything is old we reject it. Novelty has become a criterion for truth. So there is as great a phobic response to anything antiquarian in modern to novelty in classical Christian consciousness. Although one may take either of these too far, our culture errs in the direction of the idolatry of the new. Believers personally need and have a right to a living tradition of preaching, worship, and discipline."[27]

Another representative recovery theologian, David F. Wells, insists that theology must return to the church rather than be confined to the walls of academia. Wells asks, "Why is this so important? There can be no theology worthy of that name that is not a *theology for the church*, a theology in which the church actively participates, in which it understands itself to be theology's primary auditor. The church is the place where biblical knowledge must be learned, developed, and applied. The church is the context in which God and His Word should receive their most serious thought."[28]

When the recovery theologians are at their best, they call for the church to return to its heritage of teaching and preaching the Word. When they are *not* at their best, they build straw men of contemporary churches, megachurches, and the Church Growth Movement. Then, some of the recovery theologians fiercely criticize the straw men which they have built. Some of their criticisms are well-founded, indicating wisdom and discernment. Others are absurd. To summarize Bill Hybels, one wonders if the critics ever spent significant time with a hell-bound sinner.

Still the exciting contribution of the recovery theologians is that many churches are awakening to the hunger that exists for the teaching and preaching of biblical theology. The traditional church in the twenty-first century will recover its most important tradition: the Bible and the right teaching and preaching of God's Word.

## Expository Preaching

Though closely related to the contributions of recovery theologians, the renewal of expository preaching in traditional churches is a movement unto itself. Richard L. Mayhue defines expository preaching as that study and proclamation which "focuses predominantly on the text(s) under consideration along with its (their) context(s). Exposition normally concentrates on a single text of Scripture, but it is sometimes possible for a thematic/theological message or a historical/biographical discourse to be expository in nature. An exposition may treat any length of passage."[29]

Mayhue notes that exposition remains true to the biblical text, while also communicating to a contemporary world. "Exposition presupposes an exegetical process to extract the God-intended meaning of Scripture and an explanation of that meaning in a contemporary way. The biblical essence and apostolic spirit of expository preaching needs to be recaptured in the training and preaching of men who are freshly committed to 'preaching the Word.'"[30]

Expository preaching will be a key vehicle for the recovery of theology in the twenty-first century traditional church. A new generation of men and women will become grounded in the Word, unlike their parents and grandparents.

A recent analysis of sermons from two major preaching journals over a ten-year period revealed some interesting insights into modern-day preaching. The study classified the published sermons into four categories.[31]

The first category would best be called *expository* because the content of the sermons and their organization were determined by the biblical passage. Sermons in the second category included biblical content, but the preacher imposed his own organization according to his message. The biblical passage did not determine the organization.

The third group of sermons had no biblical passages to determine the content or the organization, yet the messages were identifiably Christian. And finally, the fourth category of sermons were neither biblical in their organization or content, nor did the message have any discernible Christian truths.

Less than one-fourth of these "evangelical" sermons could be classified as expository. And, surprisingly, over one-half of the sermons had *no* biblical passage as its basis for truth. It is little wonder then, among our "strongest" evangelical churches, two generations of biblical illiterates have been produced. If the spiritual leader, the preacher/pastor, is not teaching the Bible in a cogent, comprehensible, and contextual manner, how can we expect proper theology to be grasped among God's people in the church?

God's sovereignty and grace, however, has caused a new emphasis to arise. The new cry for biblical expository preaching has been heard in traditional churches across our land. By the mid-1980s the cry had certainly developed into a recognizable movement. A national Congress of Biblical Exposition (COBE) convened to encourage the church to return to sound biblical exposition. "COBE's recurring theme demanded that the American church must return to true biblical preaching or else the Western world would continue its descent toward a valueless culture."[32]

This new movement will continue to have a profound affect upon the traditional church. Earlier movements reclaimed the authority of Scripture. Now more recent developments have resulted in deeper theological teaching and preaching in our churches.

Yet we must include one more unlikely partner in the rediscovery of the Bible and theology in the traditional church. To that strange bedfellow we now turn.

## The Seeker-Church Movement

Perhaps no modern-day movement has received the amount of fierce criticism within the evangelical family as the seeker-church movement has. Bill Hybels and the Willow Creek Community Church in South Barrington, Illinois, have been the most visible targets. From Hybels' perspective, the seeker-church movement is simply an awareness that the church needs to reach the lost in its community.[33]

The critics see the movement in a different light. David Wells believes the seeker-church movement compromises the gospel by wrongly using "cultural devices."[34] John MacArthur agrees: "The simple reality is that one *cannot* follow a market-driven strategy and remain faithful to Scripture. Preachers who concern themselves with user-friendliness cannot fearlessly proclaim the whole counsel of God."[35]

Both positions have their strengths; but the issue is not as black and white as either the proponents or the critics claim. A consequence of the seeker-church movement *has* been the embracing of seeker-sensitive methodologies without a grasp of the whole counsel of God—*in some churches*. On the other hand, the movement has caused many churches in our nation to have a heightened awareness of the culture and society in which they minister. Theology does not exist in a vacuum. It exists among sin-sick cultures that need to hear—in their language—the whole gospel message.

The early church first viewed itself as a *missionary* movement. Therefore it was in the content of a missionary movement that theology was defined and articulated.[36] The contribution of the seeker-church movement is its insistence that the church of today is first a missionary movement seeking to be an instrument of God to draw people to the Savior. The seeker-church movement rallies around Paul's missionary cry that he has "become all things to all men so that by all possible means I might save some" (1 Cor. 9:22). Yet the recovery theologians rally around the same apostle's mandate to Titus: "You must teach what is in accord with sound doctrine" (Titus 2:1).

Both groups are right. But we cannot choose between a missionary zeal that uses methodologies to reach today's culture and a theological zeal that insists sound doctrine must undergird all that the church does. We must insist upon both in our churches. The traditional churches of the twenty-first century *will* reap the benefits of a new zeal for deep theological teachings. But that theological zeal will in no way hinder the church's missionary zeal. The traditional church of the next century will preach the Word *and* make disciples of all nations.

Chapter 3

# "Teach These Things . . ." ChurchTrend 3: The Renewal of the Sunday School

But unless special countermeasures are taken, the strength of a new religion tends to weaken from one generation to the next . . . There tends to be a lukewarmness in the children of believers and *their children*.

—Dean Hoge, Benton Johnson, and Donald A. Luidens

Is there a strong relationship between the quality of Sunday School programming and church growth? The answer is yes. [Sunday School is] . . . *strongly* correlated with church growth.

—C. Kirk Hadaway

SAM AND HELEN BELIEVE that everyone knows more about them than they do themselves. The couple has read and heard about their generation until they are totally exasperated with the opinions of the "experts."

Sam and Helen Drake are baby boomers — that over-studied, over-analyzed, over-discussed, and over-indulged generation. The Drakes were both born in 1955, almost the midpoint of the 1946-1964 largest generation in America's history. They have heard how their parents, with renewed optimism after the victories of World War II, decided to begin their families. Some decided on large families.

The Drakes know that when their generation moves, breathes, or makes a decision, thousands of consumer experts analyze each step, trying to determine how their companies can hawk new products to the nearly 50 million people who were born during that post-war period. No generation in the history of the world has been analyzed as much as the boomers.

The sociologists, marketers, and trend-watchers saw another major opportunity for analysis when the boomers themselves began having children. Would the indulged generation change their purchasing patterns? Would they try to raise their children differently? Would they indulge another generation in the same manner in which they were raised? Or would they desire something deeper, even spiritual, for their children?

Sam and Helen Drake know well the inner crises they have experienced with these questions. Sam and Helen had drifted from the church when they were college students. After graduating from their state universities in 1977, they married in December of that year. Their children, Josh, Lydia, and Sarah were born in 1980, 1982, and 1985.

When Josh was born, they gave some thought to the churches they left, but careers and self-fulfillment were still the priorities of their lives. By the time Sarah was born, however, they had three children, and the oldest of the three was entering kindergarten.

The parents began to have extended discussions about their children's future. Perhaps for the first time in their memories, Sam and Helen considered someone other than themselves. They realized that they were shaping a new generation — a generation that would include their own offspring, their own flesh and blood.

Josh, Lydia, and Sarah were not deficient in material needs. The best of schools awaited Josh for kindergarten and his sisters would have the same opportunity in the years ahead. But what about their deeper needs, their spiritual needs? Sam and Helen knew that even though their own superficial desires were being met, a longing—an emptiness remained—that had not been filled. They desired something more for themselves and, especially, for their children.

In late 1986, the Drake family returned to church (they would not think of exposing baby Sarah to all the childhood diseases in a nursery the year she was born). They had sought the advice and recommendation of friends and, as a consequence, chose Wendover Community Church. The church was several miles from their home, but that mattered little to the Drakes.

The initial experience was positive. Wendover's pastor, Jay Ennis, was a boomer himself. Pastor Ennis had enthusiastically studied his generation. He felt that worship services needed to be "user-friendly," so families like the Drakes would not be intimidated by strange liturgy and cold Christians.

In many ways Pastor Ennis was correct. The Drakes *did* feel that Wendover had made every effort to make them feel at home. They were very pleased with the nursery and preschool departments, which were clean, well-attended, efficient, and safety-conscious.

The worship services also pleased the Drakes. They vaguely remembered their childhood churches where visitors were required to stand and be recognized. They entered Wendover Community Church with fear and trembling, but much to their pleasant surprise, the worship service allowed the Drakes to remain anonymous. The service moved quickly and with excitement. The Drake family left Wendover that first Sunday with a new enthusiasm to return again.

Over the next four years the Drakes became more and more involved with the church. They became active in different aspects of Wendover's ministry, including an occasional stay in the church's fellowship groups (Pastor Ennis had taken the "Sunday School" label off these groups in 1985 for fear that the name might convey a negative image.). The groups were particularly helpful to the Drakes when they felt the topic covered was personally relevant. They attended for eight consecutive weeks the series, "Getting Your Finances on Track." And Sam and Helen only missed one week of the twelve-week study, "Strengthening Your Marriage for Life."

However, on one particular rainy Sunday in April of 1990, the Drakes decided to sleep in and missed all of the church's activities that day. Excuses became easier in the weeks ahead and attendance became more and more sporadic. The Drakes attended church one last time on Easter Sunday of 1991. They have not returned.

## Those Peculiar Boomers

The story of the Drakes is fictitious, although I could cite hundreds of literal examples that would be similar. Indeed, some of my own spiritual pilgrimage would not be unlike the story above (Fortunately, my story includes one of returning and not leaving).

The fascinating study of church growth and decline in the latter half of the twentieth century is tied directly to the Sunday School and the baby boom generation. Although much has been written about the relationship between the boomers and worship. I believe Sunday School may be a more vital link than that of worship.

The generation's entrance (as children in the fifties), exodus (as adolescents and adults in the sixties and seventies), and re-entrance (as adults in the eighties and nineties) have impacted the trends of

Sunday School. Indeed the fifties were a time of significant growth that has been followed by mostly steady decline. Some hope was rekindled by the return of families such as the Drakes, but the decline in Sunday School, at best, has been slowed. I believe there is a largely-unrecognized correlation between church growth and vitality and Sunday School. Therefore I make two rather bold statements. *First, the spiritual vitality of our churches in the next century will be in large part determined by the quality of the Sunday School program. Second, the American church in the twenty-first century will experience a profound renewal that will be directly correlated to a renewal of the Sunday School movement.* A very traditional element of the church will be a vital part of the renewed church in the next century! Before I begin to defend this thesis, several excursions are necessary. The first deals with our topic at hand, the baby boomers. Let us view some truths and myths about why they left the church and Sunday School, why they returned, and why they left again.

## Why the Boomers Left

It is not unusual for a generation to depart from the church for a season. Adolescence typically brings about a time of testing and, in some cases, rebellion. Youth do not always accept the values of their parents. The church has often been the first value from which youth depart. For the boomers, this trend was exacerbated for three reasons.

First, my generation, as previously noted, was probably the most indulged generation in American history. The optimism and affluence of boomer parents led to a heightened desire to give their children the best. The parents wanted for their children what they had not been given in their own childhood years.

This pattern of indulgence created one of the most self-centered generations ever. Drug abuse, sexual "freedom," protests, and an anti-establishment attitude were all manifestations and consequences of the self-centeredness. Most boomers had little understanding of self-sacrifice, agape love, and biblical virtues. For the boomers, their attitude was best conveyed in the song that included the words, "I did it my way."

It is little wonder that church became an increasingly lower priority for a generation whose values were the antithesis of the cross and sacrifice. Worship services were sometimes attended for social reasons, but there was certainly no need to attend Sunday School, too.

A second reason for the boomer departure, related to the first, was the increasing value of time. For a generation that had been taught they could "have it all" and "to go for all the gusto they could get," there was simply not enough time to do all the things they and their children "deserved." What were once privileges had now become rights and twenty-four hours was simply insufficient time to accomplish all that one needed to do.

Again, one of the first casualties on the boomers' priority list was church. More "self-gratifying" activities replaced the self-giving aspect of the church. Sunday Schools were usually an early-Sunday-morning activity. Many of the indulged generation used that time to catch up on their sleep. They were exhausted after "doing their thing" the week before.

The third reason boomers left was that the church failed them as well. Some of their claims that the church was irrelevant were on target. Although the church did not need to compromise its theology and call for discipleship, it did need to shift out of a paradigm that was largely a phenomenon of the fifties. For many boomers, the church was irrelevant *not* because the Bible was meaningless, but because thirty years had transpired since 1955. The church in general held tenaciously to methodologies that needed a fresh touch and new life.

The latter part of the twentieth century, however, witnessed an over-compensation for relevance. Some paradigms needed shifting, but some did not. The Sunday School paradigm was not a seasonal methodology. It was a blessed manner for communicating Christian essentials from one generation to another. When heavy doses of doctrinal truths were replaced with boring and simplistic lessons or needs-based studies, we began to lose a generation.

Before we continue, we should understand why Sunday School *is* so vitally important. First we need a clear understanding of what Sunday School is: It is a method for teaching, with conviction and depth, the whole counsel of biblical truths to all ages. Weak and diluted Bible stories are not true Sunday Schools. Needs-based study groups, though they have their place, are not Sunday Schools. A true Sunday School must see as its ongoing purpose the communication and teaching of the faith to all generations.

Dean R. Hoge, Benton Johnson, and Donald A. Luidens, three sociologists of mainline religion, came to this honest and compelling conclusion about the decline of mainline churches:

Our findings show that belief is the single best predictor of church participation, but it is orthodox Christian belief, and not the trends of lay liberalism, that impels people to be involved in church.[1]

Further, the sociologists stress that these beliefs *must* be communicated to the next generations:

Unless the youth are firmly socialized into its tenets and standards, the strength of the religious community will eventually ebb away."[2]

The Sunday School movement, when it is at its best, *is* the education arm of the faith for this generation and the next. When it is not at its best, it is a weak social group that has no lasting impact on generations to come.

### Why the Boomers Returned

In the eighties, I learned more about my generation than I ever dreamed possible (or that I ever cared to learn). I attended seven different conferences and seminars that specifically addressed the issue of the church reaching the baby boomers. I also read a dozen books and countless articles about America's most-studied generation. In time, I felt that I was a "boomer expert" myself. Little did I know how little I actually knew.

The experts were generally right in their assessments of the return of the boomers to church. The first major issue was that of emptiness or spiritual void in their lives. Robert Nail explains his return to the church in the early eighties: "I was really a child of the sixties — drugs, sex, rebellious behavior — you name it. When Mary and I got married, I took that same self-centered attitude into the relationship. We were both so empty. Our marriage nearly fell apart."

Robert and Mary Nail returned to church, believing that life was more than a continuous stream of pleasure-seeking activities. "The decision to return to church was relatively easy," said Mary. "What was most difficult was taking that first step — getting up on Sunday morning and going to a place where you haven't been since childhood." But neither Robert nor Mary have regretted their return to church. Mary comments, "Our marriage is getting stronger and Robert is a different person. I wish we had made this move earlier."

If emptiness and spiritual void offered one important explanation for the return of the boomers, the needs of the boomer's children became an equally important consideration. Said boomer parent Michelle Dockery, "I just wanted the best for my children, and that included right values and morals. When Rachel turned five, my husband and I made the decision to return to church."

With the emphasis on seeker-friendly worship services, designed primarily for the boomer generation, the value of Christian education, Sunday School, has been obscured. As Hoge, Johnson, and Luidens note in their studies of mainline churches, boomers *eagerly* desired Sunday School for their children in the eighties.[3] But they desired *real* Christian education, not ill-taught, lowly-emphasized, uncertain doctrines. They were looking for absolutes, something which transcended this life, something supernatural. Most of the churches, even those seeker-friendly churches, did not teach those "meaty" doctrines. So many of the boomers left the church—again.

### Why the Boomers Left Again

The great wave of boomers returning to the church proved to be transient. When they began to leave again, the experts offered their explanations. According to Hoge, Johnson, and Luidens, all of these explanations proved to be more myths than actual faults.

The first myth was that the countercultural youth of the sixties were the same anti-church generation of the eighties and nineties. The Hoge study refutes this thesis. "Our findings have made us doubt that the youth counterculture of the 1960s is a major source of mainline Protestant membership decline. We asked all the confirmands in our sample whether they had ever attended a rock concert, used marijuana, or taken part in marches or demonstrations. We found, as expected, that the baby boomers were much more likely than the pre-boomers."[4] Was there any correlation between youth rebellion and later church decline? According to the Hoge study, the answer is a clear "no." "Baby boomers who participated in the counterculture are only slightly less likely to be involved in church today. . . . church involvement of the two groups is roughly the same."[5]

The Hoge study also notes as myth three institutional theories for the loss of church membership. One is the shift of denominational policies: changes in Sunday School literature, worship formats, or even the content of hymnals. The second theory was the rejection of the church by the boomers as irrelevant (my mention of irrelevancy in the first exodus of the boomers is related to the common pattern of church exodus in adolescence and early adulthood). The third theory was the alienation of the laypeople in the church by denominational leaders.[6]

The conclusion of the study again notes that "all three institutional theories should be abandoned."[7] The church dropouts, when asked if the institutional factors affected their leaving, "most knew little or nothing about them. The criticisms we heard were directed almost exclusively at *local congregations*" rather than the denomination involved.[8]

Though the Hoge study is well respected in mainline denominations, it has received little attention in evangelical circles. I find this hard to understand. I think the results of the study should be shouted from the mountaintops. Church decline is a local church matter, not a denominational-hierarchy issue. If this is so, we must determine what particular local church issue is most responsible for decline and exodus. The study's conclusion concerning this point becomes especially exciting. Listen carefully to its words.

> To sum up, we are convinced that the basic reasons for membership decline have little to do with the issues highlighted in the ongoing conflict between liberal and conservative factions in the mainline denominations, or with complaints about particular congregations, or with participation in the counterculture. The study concludes, Rather the crisis the mainline churches face is a spiritual one. They have lost members because, over the years, beliefs have been changing.[9]

Unchurched persons are asking why they should be part of something that has so little conviction and such a weak desire to educate (dare we say indoctrinate?) the generations to come. Speaking of the Presbyterian situation, the Hoge study notes, "What active Presbyterian baby boomers have abandoned is the level of church participation of their parents, and in many cases the conviction of the exclusive truth of Christianity."[10]

The authors of the study were not kind and gentle to their fellow mainliners. "Today Presbyterians should not bemoan the lack of faith and church commitment exhibited by their youth, since they have no one to blame but themselves. No outside power forcibly pulled their children away from the faith. No conquering army or hostile missionaries destroyed the tradition. The Presbyterians made the decisions themselves, on one specific [doctrinal] issue after another, over the decades."[11]

## The Sunday School Solution

In the previous chapter I noted a rediscovery of the Bible and theology, a renewal that has its origins as far back as the fundamentalist/modernist controversy in the late nineteenth century. I also noted that the seeker-church movement, despite some overreactions within the movement, has made credible contributions by desiring to make Scripture relevant to today's society. Finally, I mentioned that expository preaching will be one of the vehicles by which this renewed vigor for theology will be transmitted to future generations.

But these contributions alone will not be sufficient to carry the doctrinal banner. There must be a comprehensive program of biblical/theological education that reaches all ages from the cradle to the grave. That is the very essence of what the Sunday School is all about. And that is why wise church leaders in the years ahead will seek to provide the very best Christian education for the people in the pews.

## A Brief Historical Excursion

The Sunday School is often misunderstood as a methodology whose time of effectiveness has ended. In a less-than-insightful analysis of the movement, one author comments that "Sunday School is becoming increasingly archaic in times when family patterns are changing . . . the name Sunday School carries much baggage; so much is forced into forty-five minutes before or after worship; people no longer are willing to devote three hours on Sunday morning . . . In time Sunday School may disappear."[12]

These comments are not uncommon. They fall into a syllogistic trap that goes something like this: (1) Traditional churches offer Sunday School. (2) Many traditional churches are declining. (3) Therefore, Sunday Schools are largely responsible for the decline of churches.

The historical reality of Sunday School is that, since its inception, it has changed methodologically in order to continue to provide doctrinal teaching to all generations. It is not that an "archaic" Sunday School has precipitated decline. The case, as the Hoge study so cogently states, is that Sunday Schools without doctrinal conviction precipitate decline. As we will see shortly in another cited study, doctrinally-renewed Sunday Schools are directly correlated to church growth.

People are willing to devote three hours on Sunday morning if they know that they are learning sound, in-depth doctrinal principles from Scripture. If Sunday School does disappear, what will replace it? What type of doctrinal Christian education for all ages will be made available?

The Sunday School movement originated in England in the late 1700s.[13] Robert Raikes, editor of the Gloucester Journal, hired teachers for impoverished children. The movement quickly moved to the United States and was aided by other forces pushing for social reform. Just before the beginning of the nineteenth century, Sunday Schools had spread to Massachusetts, New York, Pennsylvania, Rhode Island, and New Jersey.

After 1800, the purpose of Sunday School expanded to both education and evangelism. The first national Sunday School effort began in 1824. The American Sunday School Union's stated purpose was to organize, evangelize, and civilize. The Union trained leadership, published literature, and formed thousands of Sunday Schools by 1880.

Though the Sunday School movement began by educating children, in America it became the teaching, nurturing, and evangelizing arm of the church for all ages as the nineteenth century came to a close. Sunday School outreach was especially effective. By 1900, about 80 percent of all new church members first came to the church through Sunday School.

Though many denominations and churches have used Sunday School effectively in their churches, nobody has been so consistently successful at applying Sunday School principles as the Southern Baptist Convention. Early in the twentieth century, Arthur Flake and J. N. Barnett led the Sunday School focus. As this century comes to a close, Andy Anderson, Harry Piland, and Ken Hemphill are among the leaders of the movement. Two recognized leaders outside of Southern Baptist ranks, Elmer Towns and Larry Gilbert, also promote the Sunday School message today.

### Sunday School Tomorrow

Sunday School has weathered two centuries of theological and ecclesiological storms because of its primary purpose: to be the vehicle through which the truths of Scripture are taught to all generations. Contrary to the views of some of its critics, effective Sunday Schools are not archaic in their methodology. No traditional organization can survive for two centuries without methodological adaptation. Many of the effective churches of the twenty-first century will recognize the Spirit-inspired genius of this tradition. And, as a result, the Sunday School will be renewed to new heights for a new century.

## Arguments Against Sunday School

Not much church growth literature today advocates building churches through great Sunday Schools, outside of the Southern Baptist Convention writings and a few other evangelical groups. For many, Sunday School is a fixture of the past, a great tradition of previous eras. Today, some church leaders insist, a new model and a new paradigm are needed. Let us examine some of their objections to Sunday School.

### Sunday School Is an Obsolete Methodology.

"The era of Sunday School has ended," some protest. "The movement was blessed for its day, but its effectiveness paused in the fifties. Churches must change; stop pouring new wine into old wineskins."

The problem with this argument is that it makes two false assumptions. First, it assumes that Sunday School is stagnant methodologically. But, as our brief historical sketch noted, the movement underwent significant methodological changes in over two centuries. The constant since the early 1800s has been the teaching of biblical truths to all generations.

A second false assumption is the notion that Sunday Schools are failing because something is inherently wrong with the movement. The flaws in this perspective are twofold. First, many Sunday Schools are quite effective, and thousands of churches are demonstrating that effectiveness through decades of teaching, evangelism, and discipleship. Second, those churches that have ineffective Sunday Schools are often violating the very principles that make it a viable organization: biblical teachings may be diluted; ineffective teachers may be teaching; no constructive efforts of reaching others may be present; systematic Bible teaching may have been replaced with other types of group activity; or the organization may have been relegated to just another activity in the church.

### Boomers and Younger Generations are Anti-Institutional

"Because of this attitude," it is argued, "it is increasingly difficult to engender loyalty in something as institutionalized as Sunday School. We must offer alternatives that do not have the institutional 'churchiness' inherent in a Sunday School program."

Again, this line of thinking is based more upon perception than reality. Boomers are not inherently anti-institutional. The Hoge study demonstrated this truth cogently. To the contrary, boomers can become fiercely loyal to an institution if they believe it is a worthwhile organization. For many Sunday Schools, unfortunately, worthiness has been suspect because of weak convictions and inadequate teaching. That is a problem of those who lead the Sunday Schools, not the organization per se.

## Sunday Schools No Longer Offer the Strong Teaching Models of the Past

"The Bible studies are superficial; the teachers are ill-prepared. The material is not relevant."

Some of these arguments are true. But the fault lies with leadership rather than the Sunday School model.

## Today's Generations Will Not Give of Their Time to Sunday School

"Time is the boomer's most precious commodity. Because they are tugged in so many directions with so many commitments, they will no longer attend Sunday School."

Most of these facts are true, although the conclusion is wrong. Boomers and busters are incredibly busy and overcommitted. But they will give time to causes which they perceive as worthy. I have known hundreds of boomers and busters who, although as busy as any of their peers, are fiercely devoted to their Sunday School classes. Why? They are learning the Bible, ministering to others, and reaching out to the world. In other words, their participation is making a difference, so they are willing to give time to something that is life-changing for them and others.

## Cell Groups Are Replacing Sunday School Classes

"The institutionalized Sunday School methodology is being replaced with the more informally structured cell groups that meet in homes and other locations away from the church building. Unchurched and inactive church members are more likely to be open in such an atmosphere, and less intimidated by church buildings."

I must confess that I am still uncertain about the precise meaning of cell groups. Some writers define it in terms of their meeting location, i.e. away from the church building. Others define it by its informality and open atmosphere which encourages participation.

Because I have never defined Sunday School by its meeting time and location in church buildings on Sunday, it is possible that what some might call cell groups I would call Sunday School. I have defined Sunday School as the arm of the church that is concerned with teaching the whole counsel of the Bible to all generations. If this is taking place in cell groups, then the issue is simply one of terminology.

Some cell groups, however, are not concerned with continuous and systematic Bible teaching. Some focus on a particular issue: finances, marriage, raising children, etc. Others are support groups for a variety of needs. While all of these groups can be healthy for the church, they should not replace Sunday School or any similar organization that is responsible for teaching the Bible on an ongoing basis. One generation may benefit, but the church will suffer decline in future generations.

It seems that this message is now being heard. Participation in non-Sunday-school cell groups has declined precipitously.[14] Boomers now want to return to Sunday School with their families. Listen to this finding in the Hoge study:

> What do boomers want to buy that churches have to offer? . . . The most important is religious education for children and associate support for family life. We were amazed that 96 percent of the sample —including churched and unchurched — said they would like religious education for their own children! It was nearly unanimous. Almost all parents want religious education for their children, and most want to get it in Sunday Schools.[15]

Wise church leaders will heed this message. The traditional Sunday School may be both the education and outreach tool of the twenty-first century.

## Sunday School Is Restricted by Space Constraints

"Because Sunday School meets in church buildings, it is limited by the space available."

Again, this argument is based upon the false perception that Sunday School must meet in a church building. Many traditional churches have become highly innovative in finding space for new Sunday School classes. Homes, restaurants, buses, and outdoor sites are but a few examples of places where traditional Sunday Schools are meeting today.

## Arguments for Sunday School

The renewal of the Sunday School in the twenty-first century is a trend worth watching. There are four key reasons for such an optimistic view point.

### Sunday School Is the Instrument through Which Biblical Truth Is communicated

In 1972 Dean Kelley, a United Methodist minister and an executive with the National Council of Churches, published an analysis of church decline in mainline denominations in his book Why Conservative Churches Are Growing. He noted that "at least ten of the largest Christian denominations in the country, whose memberships totalled 77,666,223 in 1967, had fewer members the next year and fewer yet the year after."[16] The significance of these numbers, said Kelley, increased when one realized that a trend of 200 years had been reversed. "Most of these denominations had been growing uninterruptedly since colonial times. In the previous decade they had grown more slowly, some failing to keep pace with the increase in the nation's population. And now they have begun to diminish, reversing a trend of two centuries."[17]

The primary thesis of Kelley's work could best be summarized as "strong churches grow; weak churches decline." The "strength" to which Kelley referred was the strength of belief, or doctrinal teaching. Those churches that maintained strong doctrinal convictions and offered means by which the teachings could be communicated, were the churches that sustained long-term growth.

Kelley's thesis was debated for years, especially among mainline denominations. After two decades of discussion, the conclusion is now "we believe Kelley is right."[18] Hoge comments, "The findings from our study of Presbyterian confimands and from other recent research have convinced us that Kelley was right to describe the mainline Protestant denominations as weak and to emphasize the critical importance of belief — or 'meaning,' as he puts it — in creating and sustaining strong religious bodies."[19]

I believe a key reason for the weakening of belief in churches was the decreased emphasis on Sunday Schools with strong doctrinal convictions. Perhaps the long-term correlation in the decline of churches will be more directly related to Sunday School than any other single factor.

However, I presently see a rekindled awareness and enthusiasm for Sunday School as the critical teaching arm of the church. Look for a Sunday School renewal in the next few years.

## Sunday School Is a Good Structure for Teaching Biblical Truths

The traditional age-graded model for teaching Sunday School is a good model. Certainly it should have some inherent flexibility, but I know of no other structure that can reach all age groups as well as the age-graded format.

As we noted earlier, some churches are abandoning or decreasing their emphasis on Sunday School because they believe that boomers and post-boomers are anti-institutional. Actually, as our survey of recent studies showed, these generations appreciate structure, especially when it is well-done and well-organized. They have institutional structure in other areas of their lives — work, school, and even recreation. There is no reason to abandon good structure in the church.

## Sunday School Organization Unleashes the Laity for Ministry

The Sunday School organization is a superior tool for involving Christians in ministry. Few methodologies can offer the number of opportunities for involvment at varying levels of commitment. In our enthusiasm to find new models to unleash the laity for ministry, we should not neglect this long-standing paradigm.

## Strong Sunday Schools Are Directly Correlated to Church Growth

In the many conversations about new models for church growth, one significant study has been conspicuously overlooked. When C. Kirk Hadaway tested numerous church principles for statistical correlation to growth, he found *quality* Sunday Schools to be one of the *strongest* correlative factors.[20]

New paradigms and new models seem to be getting the most attention these days. Certainly church leaders need to be aware of the latest methodologies and trends. We need to be on the cutting edge of reaching and discipling people for Christ. But for some, embracing the new means abandoning the old. I believe many churches have made serious errors by failing to focus their resources on Sunday School.

Figure 3.1 depicts the strong relationship between a quality Sunday School ministry and church growth. Among growing churches studied by Hadaway, 84 percent rated their adult Sunday School as excellent or good; only 46 percent of declining churches did so.

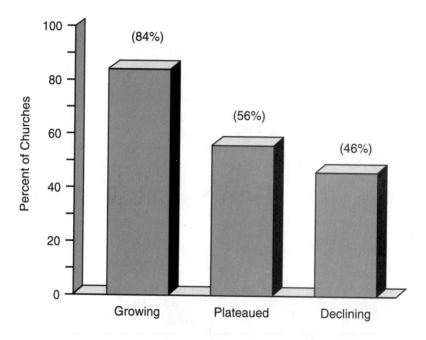

**Figure 3.1: Adult Sunday School Rated Excellent or Good**

Source: C. Kirk Hadaway, *Church Growth Principles: Separating Fact from Fiction* (Nashville: Broadman, 1991)

Hadaway comments that "having a good [Sunday School] program does not *ensure* growth, but *not* having a good program will make growth extremely unlikely."[21] He also found that those churches that work their Sunday School ministry the hardest often have the greatest growth. "Apparently, many churches are doing the 'basics' with regard to Sunday School for adults and children, but churches (even small congregations) which go *beyond* the basics to provide quality programs for *all* age groups in the church are most likely to experience growth."[22]

Hadaway's statistical analysis is in perfect agreement with the Hoge study. A *quality* Sunday School (i.e. strong biblical teachings in a well organized setting) for *all* age groups (the communication of biblical truths to all generations) will likely engender long-term growth.

It cannot be overemphasized that the Sunday School must be one of quality: in teaching, in outreach, in assimilating, and in caring. Merely filling slots with unmotivated and uncaring teachers and workers will do more harm than good. I cannot stress enough to pastors, staff persons, and lay leaders that Sunday School may very well be the organizational future for their traditional churches in the twenty-first century.

Furthermore, the Hadaway study demonstrates that renewing the emphasis on quality Sunday Schools may be the key for declining churches to become growing churches (Hadaway refers to these turnaround churches as "breakout" churches). Figure 3.2 illustrates this truth. Nearly eight out of ten breakout churches reported an increased emphasis on the Sunday School over the past several years. Said Hadaway, "Breakout churches have improved many areas of ministry in order to grow off long-standing plateaus.

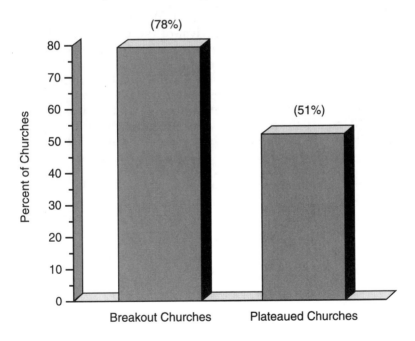

**Figure 3.2: Churches with Increased Emphasis on Sunday School**

Source: C. Kirk Hadaway, *Church Growth Principles: Separating Fact from Fiction* (Nashville: Broadman, 1991)

Sunday School is only one of these areas, *but it is apparently foundational for breakout growth.*" [23]

## The Sunday School in the Twenty-first Century

Undoubtedly different models for small groups will emerge into the next century. For example, one paradigm that is receiving an increasing level of attention is the cell group/metachurch model. Carl George of Pasadena is a leading proponent of this approach. We need to remain open to models that God is blessing or will bless in the years ahead.

Interestingly, many of the newer paradigms incorporate basic Sunday School principles. Church growth researcher John N. Vaughn notes that "metachurch dynamics include Sunday School group multiplication rather than exclude them." [24] Further, Vaughn notes, "America's fastest growing churches demonstrate that Sunday School groups continue to be the premier small-group model in the nation." [25]

The "dinosaur" is not extinct. To the contrary, the very traditional model of Sunday School that many have written off may be the model that contributes to the revival of the established church in the years ahead. But one word of caution is needed. Weak Sunday School models do more harm than good. The successful Sunday Schools of the twenty-first century will train the most capable teachers possessing the strongest convictions. They will enlist true givers of mercy and compassion to minister to the class members. They will equip those with a passion for evangelism to be the outreach arm of the Sunday School. But they will enlist only those who are committed, dedicated, and passionate about their ministries.

The traditional church is indeed a giant. And the traditional Sunday School model is a giant unto itself. But signs of awakening are imminent. Christian leaders who awaken their own sleeping giant of Sunday School may yet see the greatest days in their churches.

# Chapter 4

# "Become All Things . . ."
# Church Trend 4:
# The New Understanding of Culture

Whether these are the worst of times or the best of times, they are the only times we have.

—Art Buchwald

HERB MILLER RELATES THE STORY of Thomas Carlyle, who was dressed to speak before a large crowd one Sunday. His mother, who was sitting beside the front door, spoke to her son as he was departing. "And where might you be going, Thomas?" she asked. "Mother," he replied, "I'm going to tell the people what is wrong with the world." "Aye, Thomas," his mother responded, "but are you going to tell them what to do about it?"[1]

Western Christians live in that strange era called postmodernity, an age which acknowledges that the Enlightenment project failed. But if modernity and all of its promises failed us, what does postmodernity offer? Better stated, how can we believers make a difference in such a peculiar time?

We know, like Thomas Carlyle, that something is wrong with the world. But we are not too certain what to do about it. The novelist Walker Percy was asked what his greatest concern about our nation was. Percy responded, "Probably the fear of seeing America, with all its great strength and beauty and freedom . . . gradually subside into decay through default and be defeated, not by the Communist movement, demonstrably a bankrupt system, but from within by weariness, boredom, cynicism, greed, and in the end, helplessness before its great problems."[2]

Aleksander Solzhenitsyn expressed his concern in a recent speech: "The West . . . has been undergoing an erosion and obscuring of high moral and ethical ideas. The spiritual axis of life has grown dim."[3] And novelist John Updike said it similarly: "The fact that, compared to the inhabitants of Africa and Russia, we still live well, cannot ease the pain of feeling we no longer live nobly."[4]

The politics of this age are no less interesting. In 1992, we elected Bill Clinton as president with the key political issue being the economy ("It's the economy stupid!"). Less than two years later the economy had improved significantly, but the American populace was as discontent as ever. Why? Improved economic standards did not reverse the decaying moral trends in our nation. The people discovered that their emptiness was more spiritual than financial.

Issachar was unique among the twelve tribes of Israel. The tribe was an agricultural people who spent long, hard days working the soil. Their hard work resulted in abundant crops. The Bible tells of the pleasant land of Issachar and the tribe's desire to work the land (Gen. 49:14–15).

Tradition has it that Zebulun and Issachar agreed to devote time to the areas in which their people were most gifted and talented. Zebulun would take on the tasks of commercial interest, and Issachar would spend time in prayer and study of the Torah.[5]

Another brief passage of Scripture about Issachar is likewise fascinating. And it would seem to fit well in that story from Genesis. The context of the passage is the numbering of men fighting for David's kingdom. They met at Hebron ready to turn Saul's kingdom over to David (1 Chron. 12:23). The count was made of the fighting men, tribe by tribe (1 Chron. 12:24–37). Seventh on the list were the "men of Issachar, who understood the times and knew what Israel should do" (1 Chron. 12:32).

The tribe of Issachar had studied and thus understood the times and culture in which they lived. Consequently, they knew the direction they should go. I believe that God is raising up "men of Isachaar" today, men and women who are studying the times for the church, who are suggesting that God is showing us where the church should go. I believe the traditional church in America will hear more clearly these voices with each passing day. And, as a result, the traditional church will make a salt-and-light difference in our strange culture.

But, for a moment, let us take a brief excursion and look at two churches. Both churches are real. The name of the first has been changed for obvious reasons.

# A Tale of Two Churches

## First Church, Deep South

In this story we turn our attention to Jess Dutton. He is typical of the many active members at First Church, at least until now.

Jess has recently been challenged by his Sunday school's study of the book of Acts. He is particularly fascinated with the early chapter, where the Christians' lifestyles are drawing people to the Savior (Acts 2:42–47). Jess decides to visit Pastor Lewis and share the sense of conviction that God wants Jess to do something beyond his routines at church. The meeting takes place on Thursday of the next week.

"Greetings, Jess!" Pastor Lewis exclaims as Jess enters his study. "What is the honor of this visit?"

"Ben," Jess quickly gets to the point, "God is really speaking to me. We recently completed Acts in Sunday School, and I am convinced that most of the Christians at First Church don't have a clue about what it means to be salt and light in this world. I recently walked six blocks west of our church building and saw at least a dozen people with very obvious needs. Ben, you know as well as I do that most of these people don't even know First Church exists. We've got to do something!"

The pastor of fourteen years is taken back by the middle-aged corporate executive. Though the two of them are not close friends, they have always had a genuine respect for one another during the twelve years of their acquaintance. Ben is shocked to see Jess out of his quiet, conservative demeanor. This is a side his pastor has not seen.

"What do you suggest?" the pastor asks. Jess responds honestly, "I don't know, Ben. I guess that's why I'm here. The possibilities are endless though. We know that there are quite a few transients around here. We could provide a shelter and food for them. Or we could provide some kind of counseling center and home for all the abused women we read about right in our neighborhood. Boy, we could really have an evangelistic thrust.

Or we . . ."

"Jess, Jess, slow down!" the pastor interrupts. "You're moving too fast. Look, I admire your enthusiasm. But let's get real for a moment. You've been at First Church almost as long as I have. You know the people here. Change is not accepted quickly. I'll be honest with you, Jess. We would have a big problem if we tried to do anything like you suggested."

You can see the enthusiasm draining from Jess. He asks slowly, "Is there anything I can do . . .?"

The pastor thinks for a moment. "I've got an idea. Riverview Church is sending a team of men and women to the neighborhoods around us to work on some of these decaying homes. You know, plumbing, roof repairs, insulation . . . things like that. You know the pastor, Mike Stewart. Why don't you give him a call? I'm sure he would welcome the help. He wanted our church to be partners with his church, but I told him that our folks weren't quite ready for something like that."

Less that two months later, Jess is standing before the people of First Church in the monthly business meeting. He shows slides of the work that the Riverview team did. He shares his own testimony of leading a fourteen-year-old drug addict to Christ and of finding a good foster home for the boy. "Folks," Jess pleads. "This past week I have tasted the Christian life as it was meant to be. I have seen what a church can do when, in Christ's power, it decides that the status quo is not enough. First Church *must* begin opening our doors and hearts to the hurting and lost in our own neighborhoods. I plead with you to seek God's guidance for our next step."

Those First Church members who were in attendance were obviously moved by the sincerity and conviction they sensed in Jess Dutton. A lengthy time of discussion ensued. Perhaps the largest block of time was spent discussing what would happen if "those kind of people" actually came into their church facility. Betty Wright was particularly concerned about the new carpet.

A motion was finally made, seconded, and passed. The church would have a special mission offering to send to Riverview Church for their ministry in the area. Within a few weeks Jess and his family left the church to join Riverview.

## Celebration Christian Fellowship, Tacoma, Washington

The wire report came across my desk. It was one among dozens of religious news items I receive weekly in my position as a seminary dean. The majority of the reports receive a cursory glance, but this one got my attention.

"In a day of aggressive church marketing, Celebration Christian Fellowship runs counter to some church trends as well as to secular society," the report began.[6] "Rather than developing a marketing strategy for reaching an affluent suburb, Celebration members focus on becoming stronger Christians while operating a dozen lay-led ministries in some of Tacoma's toughest communities."

Celebration's growth has come primarily from conversion, many of whom are former convicts and addicts. Says pastor Jay Chambers, "People aren't hard to reach, if you don't care who you catch." The pastor runs a gift, flower, and antique shop to support the church's ministry. With the type of people the church is reaching, they need more financially than they can give, at least initially.

Pastor Chambers had read a lot of the material about the uncommitted baby boomers. But he believes commitment comes when the cause is Christ. What does it take to become a member of Celebration? Commitment includes, among other things:

- a daily Bible reading and prayer time;

- a minimum giving of a tithe;

- weekly reconciliation to anyone with whom you are unreconciled;

- a minimum involvement of two hours Christian service each week.

The new members actually sign commitment cards to agree to these items. The pastor views this method as Celebration's way of being counter to culture, like the church at Jerusalem, where members sold their possessions and had all things in common (Acts 2:44–45).

The stories of Celebration's counter-cultural (biblical!) revolution abound. One person's crisis becomes the church's ministry. Over six thousand dollars has been raised for alcohol treatments alone. The members also commit to avoid strife in church business. "We don't have business meetings," the pastor notes. "We pray till we all feel in one accord about it."

An unwed couple were fugitives from the police. They came to Celebration with their baby seeking sanctuary, so the church began ministering to the couple. When the police visited Pastor Chambers and learned what had taken place, they said, "Well, see what you can do with them." Within a few months the couple became Christians, got married, and joined the church. The father now has a regular job in a restaurant.

Some of the members sensed God's leading to start a home for unwed, pregnant teen-agers. But the church was financially unprepared when a nine-bedroom house in the community went on the market. The house last sold for $102,000, but the church, in an act that seemed foolish to some, offered $40,000. The seller counter-offered for $35,000!

Stories of miracles abound. A logger from nearby Buckly felt called to pastor a mission congregation. But he was dyslexic and could not read anything. The church members laid hands upon him and prayed that God would heal him. Most of the members, the pastor admits, forgot about that prayer in the months that followed. But it was then that the man stood in front of the church and read from the Bible flawlessly. To this day he cannot read anything but the Bible.

Pastor Chambers confesses that no grand long-range plan or extraordinary methodology is in place at Celebration Christian Fellowship. "When our people think that Jesus says, 'Do this,' they just try to do it."

So what is the difference between First Church and Celebration Christian Fellowship? It lies in the attitude of the people. At first Church, the people see themselves largely as ineffective. When their faith does make a difference in the culture, they see it as the exception rather than the rule. At Celebration, the people see their faith as a daily challenge to the standards of the culture in which they live.

The story of Celebration Christian Fellowship should not be unusual or extraordinary. It should be typical. Perhaps it will be the norm in the twenty-first century.

## Where Is the Church Today?

Most of us who are forty-plus can recall a time when Christian values were normative in our country. I was born in 1955 and have vivid memories of Bible readings and prayer in the public school I attended. I remember how discreetly Lucy's pregnancy was handled on "I Love Lucy." What a contrast to the implicit and explicit sexual mores on television today!

I also remember the church as the most respected institution in town, with the pastor, in most cases, among the most respected people. Though divorces took place among a few of my peers' parents, I remember the terrible social stigma attached to the broken family. And I can recall knowing only one peer who was born to unmarried parents.

If I seem to be taking a syrupy, sentimental journey down memory lane, forgive me. I know that my memory of the first six to eight years of my life is selective. Families did have problems then. The church was not experiencing an Acts-like revival. And the immorality of some men in my hometown was quietly applauded —they, after all, were the sexual "conquerors."

Still, those first few years of my life were lived in a society where the values were known. Even if immorality was ignored or winked at, the townspeople knew that a rule had been broken. The values, the rules, the norm, the mores — whatever you call it — were known because they had been written down for two or more millennia. The ethical standard was the Bible. And you accepted that standard whether you were a believer or unbeliever, whether you complied or violated it. Adultery was a broken rule regardless of one's obedience or disobedience. Everyone knew that the Bible prohibited it, and so the norm was accepted.

But today, marriage and its responsibilities are seen in an entirely different light. The most popular view of the day is the so-called "standard." Once built upon the unchangeable source of God's Word, marriage now sits precariously on the shifting sands of postmodern confusion.

James Q. Wilson of the University of California, Los Angeles, explains this new foundation for marriage:

> The contemporary legal system views people as autonomous individuals endowed with rights and entering into real or implied contracts. The liberalization of laws pertaining to marriage and divorce arose out of just such a view.[7]

He goes on to explain how different this foundation of marriage has become compared to just a few years earlier:

> Marriage, once a sacrament, has become in the eyes of the law a contract that is easily negotiated, renegotiated, or rescinded. Within a few years, no-fault divorce on demand became possible, after millennia in which such an idea would have been unthinkable. It is now easier to renounce a marriage than a mortgage; at least the former occurs much more rapidly than the latter. Half of all divorced fathers rarely see their children, and most pay no child support.[8]

In years past we expected the church to take a firm stand opposing those antibiblical values; today we see a church that is largely silent. The Western church of the late twentieth century will be remembered as the church that bowed down before the god of culture.

Now some may point to significant growth and influence in some churches. Admittedly, not all churches are idolaters of culture. But an honest assessment of the Western church in general cannot be too favorable. Charles Colson notes: "While the church may seem to be experiencing a season of growth and prosperity, it is failing to move people to commitment and sacrifice. The hard truth is that we have substituted an institutionalized religion for the life-changing dynamic of a living faith."[9]

Colson is no less critical of the church when he assesses the less-than-powerful impact it has had on culture. "When compared with previous generations of believers, we seem among the most thoroughly at peace with our culture, the least adept at transforming society, and the most desperate for a meaningful faith. Our *raison d'etre* is confused, our mission obscured, and our existence as a people in jeopardy."[10]

How did our nation so quickly change from a people whose values were based on absolutes to an immoral culture so powerful that many churches were overcome? Was it a transformation of only a few years? Or did the change come slowly, after decades or centuries of cultural shifts? Actually, both are true. Let us take a brief historical look where we have been, so that we might better know where we are going.

## A Historical Sketch of Culture

Leonard Sweet tells the story of a conversation between his colleague Gordon Goodgame and a friend: "An old friend dropped by my study one day. We entered seminary together, I just twenty one and he in his forties responding to a call to ministry . . .. Twenty-two years later, we talked of his struggles in ministry, and he buried his head in his hands and cried. He said, 'This is just not the world we were trained to serve in.'"[11]

What then is this world? In some ways it defies definition. In other ways it is a clear break from the past of absolutes and virtue. Sweet states that it would be an exaggeration to say that the cultural divide is so wide that it has become a chasm where communication is all but impossible. "What would not be an overstatement," says Sweet, "is the assertion that the flux and fragmentation of end-of-the millennium living is a part of a . . . paradigm shift not unlike that from Roman paganism to Christianity in the fourth century."[12]

We can examine this historical moment through the history of ideas. The seventeenth-century scientific revolution and the eighteenth-century Enlightenment celebrated the accomplishments of humanity. Whether in the arts or sciences, the focus began to tilt toward human-centeredness rather than God-centeredness. In America, the shift was so gradual for nearly two hundred years as to be almost imperceptible. Then the ramifications of humanity-centeredness began to sweep our nation like a tidal wave.

The cultural shift has been most noticeable during the eras called modernity and postmodernity of the twentieth century. Modernity, as defined by Os Guinness, is the "character and system of the world produced by the forces of modernization and development."[13] Modernity is a natural continuation of humanity's accomplishments in earlier centuries.

But more than just a celebration of accomplishments, modernity became dependent on such accomplishments. Perhaps in a spiritual sense, Western civilization began to worship modernity. Science, government, medicine, and on and on . . . these were seen as the hope for humankind. The great projects of science and Enlightenment came to their most significant fruition when men and women cried to the gods of advancement to make their lives healthier, safer, more convenient, and more entertaining.

As we approach the end of a decade, century, and millennium, the great project is failing. All the advancements engineered by humanity have failed to give our culture what it was demanding: peace, joy, and painlessness. Today the hearts of most persons are emptier; lives are less fulfilling. All the promises of the good life have been broken again and again.

Since modernity has failed, it is correct in some fashion to label our age as a new era. Thus some have simply called the period of the eighties and nineties "postmodernity," recognizing the experiment of modernity has failed, but lacking a clear identity for the age in which we live.

We must acknowledge, as Guinness insists, that the impact of modernity is still strong and pervasive. "Modernism as a set of ideas may well have collapsed," says Guinness. "And 'postmodern' may therefore be legitimate to describe the set of ideas that succeeds it. But to be postmodern in the structural sense is yet inconceivable."[14]

In the strictest sense of the definition, then, our era is "postmodern modernity," an obvious paradox whose label is as confusing as the times in which we live. And what is most confusing about this era is its lack of a belief system. Though modernity removed God from its values, the period at least had a religion that applauded the virtues of humanity and the species' accomplishments. Postmodernity no longer puts its faith in humanity; neither has it returned to the God of the Bible. Perhaps the best we can do for a definition of this era is to say that it's *after* modernity.

The impact of modernity upon our nation today can best be understood by a brief historical sketch of the last half of the twentieth century.

## The Fifties

The decade of the fifties was, at least on the surface, a time of stability.[15] Predictions of social stability gave the nation a renewed sense of optimism and hope. Divorce rates had peaked in 1946 and declined steadily throughout the fifties. "In the 1950s, American institutions from families up through public schools, law courts, and the military to the presidency itself appeared strong, inspiring both confidence and pride."[16]

The Christian worldview was still dominant. The public's confidence in the above institutions was, to a large extent, congruent with Christian values, whether they were understood in that light or not. But many did understand the Christian values explicitly. By 1955, church membership had increased from 70 million to over 100 million in just one decade.[17]

The fifties also saw a postwar attitude for hope in the institutions of society. The government, the institutional church, the military, the education system . . . these were the promises for tomorrow. The human-centered seeds of hope were about to blossom, or at least much of society perceived it so. Never in American history had so much hope been placed in human institutions.

## The Sixties

Faith in human-made institutions is a fragile faith. If trust in the ways of humanity reached an all-time high in the fifties, it was challenged and ultimately destroyed in the sixties.

Not all people shared the optimistic view of the fifties, especially people excluded from the American dream. Cafe sit-ins began in 1960. Riots broke out in southern universities, most notably the University of Mississippi in 1962. The feminist challenge was led by Betty Friedan and her landmark book, *The Feminist Mystique* in 1963. Bob Dylan led us to question institutions as we sang together that all of the answers were "Blowing in the Wind." And then the institution of the presidency was hit a crushing blow with the shot that was heard around the world on November 22, 1963. That same year, in the months of May, June, and July, 750 riots erupted in 186 cities.[18]

The institutions of marriage and the family were rocked as well. The astronomical rise in divorce and illegitimate birth rates began in 1968. The institution of the military was torn apart as never before. Vietnam became the symbol of a new hatred of the armed forces.

And if our political institutions had not already received enough blows, the assassinations of Martin Luther King and Robert Kennedy sent the nation reeling. America had lost its innocence and moral direction. Not only did the American dream appear dead, a crisis of culture seemed unstoppable and irreversible.

## The Seventies

The defining moment of one of the most undefining decades in history was the OPEC oil crisis in 1973. The last of the institutions, the economy, came tumbling down. The gloom and uncertainty from that crisis still has not lifted as we prepare to enter a new century.

Even though 1973 was also the year of Watergate and Roe v. Wade, these events were not as defining as OPEC. The institutions of politics and morality had already suffered devastating blows; Watergate and Roe were more consequences of decline than reasons behind the fall.

The seventies were years of questions. A conservative resurgence had begun, both religiously and politically, with the media declaring a new "born again movement," or what *Newsweek* called in 1976 "The Year of the Evangelical."

Jimmy Carter's election in 1976 was not a reversal of this trend as much as an affirmation of it. His victory was, first, the aftermath of Watergate but, secondly, a strong showing of support among evangelicals (for example, Pat Robertson). His defeat in 1980 was a clear signal that the Carter years proved to the evangelicals that he was not "one of us." The conservative movement wanted to stop the crisis of America's cultural authority. The decade of the eighties would be their moment in history.

## The Eighties

Regardless of one's political point of view, the decade of the eighties will most likely be remembered as the Reagan years. For some, the Reagan years meant greed and deficits; for others it was prosperity and strength.

The Cold War was won in the eighties. Defense buildup meant the development of intermediate missiles in Western Europe, the push for a Strategic Defense Initiative, and the support of anti-Communist rebels around the world. The "evil empire" came tumbling down.

Impressive gains were made in the economy. The eight years of the Reagan administration were part of the longest peacetime expansion in the nation's history. The inflation rate of 1980 had been cut by one-half. Unemployment was at a fifteen-year low with the creation of nearly 16 million new jobs. Ronald Reagan's significant accomplishment was that of no other postwar president: declines in both inflation and unemployment. And this notable accomplishment was done while tax rates were lowered. The negative legacy Reagan left was a much larger budget deficit and a new trade deficit.

But before we stray too far from our subject of culture, we must ask the questions of the eighties' legacy in this arena. It seems that the euphoric economic climate led, in some ways, to a personal demand for instant gratification. Consumer debt rose to an all-time high as marketeers told us we could "have it all today." And rightly so, we thought. We deserve it.

What the eighties actually taught us was that a return to the economy's good old days did not fill the void and emptiness in our lives. America had experienced a cultural revolution, a counter-revolution, and a counter-counter-revolution, but our hope was still misplaced. Human-made devices and institutions could never take the place of a personal God.

Our culture in the nineties realizes there must be something more, but that "something" is not defined. The New Age, preoccupation with angelic beings (not to deny the reality of biblical angels), and a growing religious pluralism and cultism are all vain attempts to fill the void. The church has its greatest opportunity in centuries to offer the one true Hope. But the church must be different, counter-cultural, and demanding of discipleship if that opportunity will be realized.

## The Church in the Culture . . . Thus Far

The church's response to the cultural confusion has been anemic thus far. Most churches still live comfortably in the age of modernity; many actually embrace the false hope of modernity. Only a few consider the implications of living in the postmodern era.

That the Western church has largely defaulted to culture can be seen in three main compromises that are somewhat overlapping. But the church's awareness of these compromises, and discussion of new paths, gives hope that the twenty-first century church may indeed be counter-cultural.

## Theological Compromise

The theological compromise of the church to the culture comes in two forms. First is the rejection of the total truthfulness of Scripture. Because modernity claims through its science and other tools that a Bible cannot be inerrant, we cower to the god of cultural authority. In doing so, we lose our base of certitude, our moral and theological compass.

Secondly, the church may confess a totally-authoritative Scripture, but practice little of its demands. Discipleship is diluted. Evangelism is ignored. Programs and routines take on a greater priority than living as servants of Christ.

In the first case, orthodoxy has been rejected. In the second case, orthodoxy has been claimed but not practiced. One is liberalism; the other is dead orthodoxy.

## Moral Compromise

A visitor to this strange land called America may understand, to some extent, the moral degeneration of our society. He or she may comprehend a social history that explains our decline. But the visitor will probably be shocked to see that the churches are little different from the culture they have been called to change. Divorce rates in both evangelical churches and society in general are similar. Teen pregnancy rates are not significantly different. And, perhaps more importantly, attitudes about moral issues are not too far apart.

*Why,* the visitor may wonder, *are the churches so much like their culture? Are they not required to live according to their Bible which calls for radically different lifestyles and attitudes?*

The relationship between theological compromises and moral compromises is close. Once one departs from the standards of an absolute, God's Word, the slippery slope inevitably leads to compromises culturally and morally.

## Methodological Compromise

In the previous chapter we mentioned that some evangelical churches have come under intense criticism by fellow evangelicals because of the church's adoption of secular methodologies without close theological scrutiny.

The desire of the seeker movement and the user-friendly movement is to relate to unbelievers who might be turned off by traditional churches methodologies, worship services, language, hymns, and religious symbols. Their desire, like the apostle Paul, is to "become all things to all men so that by all possible means I might save some" (1 Cor. 9:22).

Understanding the times, as the Issachar tribe did, is critical. When such a desire is the motive, and theology is not compromised, the task is not only admirable, it is biblically obedient.

The compromise comes when the whole counsel of biblical truth is short-changed. John MacArthur is a frequent critic of the seeker-church movement. I believe he sometimes assumes wrongly that *most* contemporary churches compromise methodologically. Still, his words and warnings are worth heeding to those churches that are methodological compromisers. MacArthur says, "But in fact the truth of Scripture is being compromised if it is decentralized and if in order to forge a friendship with the world hard truths are avoided, vapid amusements are set in place of sound teaching, and semantic gymnastics are employed to avoid mention of the difficult truths of Scripture."[19]

Though we seek to understand our culture, our task is not to make the unbeliever comfortable. MacArthur continues, "If the design is to make the seeker comfortable, isn't that rather incompatible with the biblical teaching on sin, judgment, hell, and several other important topics?"[20]

MacArthur then places the greatest responsibility with the pastor/preacher: "The weakness of the pulpit today does not stem from frantic cranks who harangue about hell; it is the result of men who compromise and who fear to speak God's Word powerfully, with conviction. The church is certainly not suffering from an overabundance of forthright preachers; rather it seems glutted with men pleasers" (Gal. 1:10).[21]

## The Reasons for an Optimistic Future

History shows that the Western church has been shaped too much by the powers of modernity. As a result few churches are living the radical demands of discipleship. Why then would I or anyone else hold the optimistic view that positive change is just a few years away?

In the next few pages I will attempt to be a voice for hope in the Western church, a voice that is in a noticeable minority. My primary reason for hope is that the cumulative impact of the return to prayer, the Bible, and a means to educate future generations will enable the church to become the counter-cultural force that God intended.

As we awaken each new day to the power of prayer and God's Word, new lifestyles that reject culture's false hopes are inevitable. Furthermore, Christians will have a greater desire and burden to reach the lost and unchurched. This will demand that we become "Isachaars" while living lifestyles that make us salt and light. Our traditional churches will understand that the best "tradition" is the historic church that attracted the pagan world through the obedience of Christians to costly discipleship.

Signs of a counter-cultural awakening are present among us now. Let us examine these signs briefly.

## We Are Becoming "Issachars"

The traditional church owes a debt of gratitude to nontraditional churches. The seeker-church movement may have its weaknesses, but it has taught us that we must be well-informed and sensitive to the cultures in which we live.

Cultural awareness and sensitivity has long been understood as a requisite to foreign missions. One cannot expect to reach a culture for Christ unless that culture is studied and understood. For many years America was basically a Western Christian culture. Such is not the case any more. The values of America are not the values of the Bible. We must understand this postmodern culture if we are to have any impact upon it.

I recently spoke with the pastor of a medium-sized traditional church that has no intentions of changing its emphasis on Sunday School and expository preaching. But the pastor is reading everything he can on American culture. "I am asking for God's wisdom," he said, "in understanding this crazy world we live in. My church must somehow, someway get the gospel to the lost people in our community. We intend to find out how to reach them."

## We Have Become Aware of Compromises

Because the call to discipleship is so radical, the church cannot compromise that call in its desire to be seeker friendly. While the nontraditional church led the way in cultural sensitivity, traditional church theologians have responded with calls for theological integrity.

As previously noted, some churches' enthusiasm to be user-friendly has resulted in a diluted gospel. The debate and exchange between recovery theologians and seeker-church leaders is healthy. Such an open discussion will result in biblical balance. Let us pray that, in our desire to speak of perceived needed corrections, we always do so in Christian love and humility. Each side (though I am hesitant to divide two evangelical perspectives into "sides") has its strengths and weaknesses. Let us listen with prayer and an open heart. And let us learn to listen twice as much as we speak.

### We Are Emphasizing the Antithesis between Christianity and Secularism

A number of evangelical scholars are bringing to a new awareness the importance of challenging non-Christian worldviews. The late Francis Schaeffer, Carl F. H. Henry and, on a popular level, Charles Colson, have highlighted the fundamental differences between Christianity and secularism.

We often view 2 Corinthians 6:14 as a mandate for Christians not to marry outside their faith: "Do not be yoked together with unbelievers." But the latter portion of the passage emphasizes the broader perspective of the issue, that the Christian should not compromise with the culture of the world: "For what do righteousness and wickedness have in common? Or what fellowship can light have with darkness?" Paul then cites a mandate from the Lord that we must not be of the world: "'Therefore come out from them and be separate, says the Lord. Touch no unclean thing, and I will receive you'" (2 Cor. 6:17).

The number of evangelical leaders calling for corporate holiness or separation is encouraging. The influence of these evangelicals is growing and impacting the church. Chuck Colson's book *The Body* was a Christian bestseller in 1992. Listen to these promotional words on the book jacket:

> There is a growing discontent with [a] low view of the Body of Christ. Christians of every tradition know the church is more than buildings, budgets, and buses. Down deep we long for a fresh vision of its role . . .[We seek] practical answers to how the church can break out of her cultural captivity and reassert her biblical identity.[22]

The momentum is growing. As we turn to a new century, increasing numbers of traditional churches will make decisions to be the Body of Christ that God intended her to be. We may very well see a countercultural revival that has had no equal since the early church.

## We Are Emphasizing the Doctrine of Sin

Some seeker churches have admittedly minimized the doctrine of sin. Critics have rightly spoken of the need for adjustments. Seeker-movement churches, however, were not the only churches to hear that message. Many traditional church leaders began to look for the needed balance in their own teaching and preaching.

One traditional-church pastor shared with me that he had been a frequent critic of the seeker-church movement. As he railed against the dilution of the gospel evident in these churches, he began to examine his own preaching. As he glanced through his sermons of the past year, he saw only one that, as he put it, "took sin seriously."

Evangelical theologian Millard J. Erickson put it this way:

> When we minimize sin, urging people to believe and follow Jesus, but failing to place a concomitant emphasis upon repentance, we are in danger of proclaiming the sort of cheap grace that Dietrich Bonhoeffer wrote about in *The Cost of Discipleship*. Grace is cheap when we are not required to negate our sinfulness. Discipleship is easy when sin and consequently repentance are minimized.[23]

## A Return to Tradition and Basics

Two major streams of influence related to the church and culture are touching the church today. One stream says to know your culture, to be an Isachaar. The other stream says to be counter-cultural in your faith. Both are right. Both are biblical.

One of the very basic traditions of the church is to be a light in the community. Unfortunately that light has often blended into the culture rather than shine brightly and differently. But a new trend bears watching. Churches across America are no longer satisfied with the sameness and the lameness of their ministries and testimonies. Some traditional churches may change to a more contemporary model, believing that will help them be more effective in the culture. But other traditional churches will hold on to many of their traditions while seeking to be light and salt in their communities of darkness. With renewed emphasis on prayer and God's Word, the traditional church of the twenty-first century may indeed change the world and culture for Christ as a small band of believers did some two thousand years ago.

# Chapter 5

# "To Prepare God's People . . ." ChurchTrend 5: The New Traditional Church Layperson

Nearly five hundred years after the Reformation there are rumblings in the church that appear to be creating a climate for something so powerful we can call it a New Reformation. The New Reformation seeks nothing less than the radical transformation of the self-perception of all believers so we see ourselves as vital channels through whom God mediates his life to other members of the body of Christ and the world.

— Greg Ogden

THE CARTOON HAS TWO OBSERVANT birds perched on a telephone wire high over the community. The largest building below is a magnificent edifice which is obviously a church. One bird comments to the other: "Yes, it's quite a nest, but they only use it once a week."

If some members of the early church were able to transport themselves forward into the twentieth century, they would most likely find the American church scene a terrible plight. Whereas the early church gladly met daily, their twentieth-century contemporaries often complain about giving two to three hours on Sunday morning. While the first-century believers sold all their possessions when a need arose, today's Christians give an average of three percent of their income. The early church saw people won to Christ daily, as their Spirit-filled lifestyles drew people to them and then to the Savior. A majority of today's believers do not share their faith even once a year. If you asked a first-century church member for their definition of "church," he or she would undoubtedly speak of an exciting body of believers living and dying daily for their Savior. The twentieth-century counterpart would likely tell you that First Baptist Church is a location, a building, on Main Street and Elm.

The birds are right! We have many magnificent buildings, "nests," but we gather in our nests, most of us anyway, once a week. When and how did we lose our biblical understanding of the church? Do we have any hope of regaining the dynamics of the early church? I believe the answers to these questions are an exciting "yes." Though many may have missed it, there has been a revolution taking place in the church. Somewhere in the 1960s, when our nation was in the turmoil of the Vietnam War, campus protests, assassinations, and racial unrest, God's Spirit began moving in an extraordinary manner. He began speaking to the person in the pew about his or her ministry in the Kingdom. Millions have responded.

Perhaps the most amazing aspect of this massive revolution has been the *lack* of attention it has received. Millions of Christians have decided that their place in God's Kingdom is one of ministry in their churches, workplaces, schools, and homes. But neither *USA Today*, *Newsweek*, *U.S. News and World Report*, nor *Time* have yet to note the movement as a news item worthy of space in their publications.

In Christian publishing circles, several books and articles have been written on the subject. The ministry of the laity has been a topic discussed from several different perspectives. Still the "unleashing of the laity" has not been recognized as the revolution it truly has become, even in the larger evangelical community. There are reasons for this great omission, which we will discuss shortly. For now, let us accept the premise that a Christian laypeople revolution began in the traditional church in the 1960s, and it is growing in churches of all types today. We will support his thesis shortly, after our visit with Marge and Jill.

### Two Persons/Two Stories

Marge and Jill were life-long friends. Theirs was the unusual story of two people who went to the same elementary school, high school, and college, where they were roommates. Their parents were also the best of friends, so the two families often ended up in the same places. Among those places was Asbury Methodist Church, where both families were active. The two women were not only raised in good Christian homes, their church provided a healthy and active Christian environment during their childhood and youth years.

Upon graduation from college, the two friends were confronted with a difficult situation. Their career choices mandated they move to different towns. For the first time in their lives the two would be separated. Marge and Jill had been nicknamed "the twins" by their peers and the description was accurate. More than most sisters, their interests, tastes, and spiritual development were remarkably similar.

On this early summer day in June, the two women bid a tearful farewell to each other. Embraces and promises of a quick reunion are shared. The time has come. Rental vans are loaded. Marge and Jill see the distance separating them in the diminishing view of their cars' rear-view mirrors.

Marge is headed to the largest city in the state, where the medical school is located. She is fulfilling her dream of becoming a pediatric surgeon. She knows that the studies and pressures will be demanding, but Marge is ready and willing. She also made a commitment to be active in a church, though time pressures will be great.

Within a few weeks Marge is a member of Faith Methodist Church, a medium-size church in an eastern suburb. One requirement for joining the church is a three-hour membership class. In the class, the associate pastor explains the importance of every-member ministry. You are not to join a church to observe, he notes. You must be prepared to serve.

After a short Bible study on laity ministry, the associate pastor asks every prospective member to complete an interests' survey and a spiritual-gifts inventory. These instruments, he says, will be used to evaluate ministry possibilities for each of them. They will be contacted later.

Within a week Marge is contacted by a member of Faith Methodist who identifies her ministry as one of administering the lay-ministry program. She explains the results of the survey and inventory. It appears that Marge has the gifts of evangelism and mercy, according to the spiritual gifts inventory. And the survey answers all point to some type of ministry with children.

Marge is amazed! She has always had a sense of deep empathy for people and a burning desire to share her faith with them as well. But her life's passion has always been to work with children.

The church member suggests that Marge may want to be involved with Faith's "God's Child/Our Child" ministry. Church members commit to spend a certain amount of time with foster children in the city. Marge determines that, with the demands of medical school, she will give three hours a week to the ministry. But before she actually begins the ministry, she is asked to spend some time with the children's minister to be equipped in the evangelism of children.

One year later Marge is an active, happy member of Faith Methodist. Her time pressures are great, but she could not be happier in her medical training or her new ministry.

Jill's path is significantly different. She moves immediately into the world of corporate business where her career path offers many opportunities for advancement. The medium-sized city is the location of the corporation's regional headquarters. Within weeks on the job, fellow workers are predicting that Jill will manage the office in the near future.

Like Marge, Jill does not forsake her commitment to her Lord and His church. She joins First Methodist Church. Membership is easy: Jill simply requests that her membership in her hometown church be transferred to First Methodist. Nothing else is required.

The people at First Methodist are friendly, but Jill seeks something more. She does not just want to go to church; she wants to do ministry within the church. When Jill mentions this desire to a newly-found friend, the friend agrees to tell the chairperson of the nominating committee. That chairperson contacts Jill within a few weeks about "an opening to teach fourth-graders." In her desire to do *anything*, Jill agrees.

Two months later, Jill knows that she has made a mistake. She does not want to teach or to work with children. She decides to complete the three months remaining in the church year, but declines to continue beyond that point.

With her involvement in church diminishing, Jill finds that her work fills that time void. With longer hours given to work, the church takes on less and less importance. It becomes amazingly easy to sleep in on Sundays. Within one year Jill is yet another casualty added to the ranks of inactive members.

## Good News/Bad News

The stories of Marge and Jill are fictitious, but the essence of their stories is true. Two women who had such similar backgrounds take very different paths in Christian ministry and church involvement. Their stories are the stories of millions of Christians in America. Some are dropping out of church. Others are becoming true lay ministers, with high levels of involvement. Fortunately, it is the latter group whose ranks will be swelling. The revolution to which I referred earlier is changing the landscape of the church and, as a consequence, our nation.

What has transpired to cause so many people to become involved in dynamic Christian ministry? The answer is one of both good news and bad news. An army of Christians are mobilizing (good news) in response to the deterioration of our nation and society (bad news).

Prior to the 1960s, though we were by no means a Christian nation, our values were determined largely by the values of Judeo-Christians morals. At least externally, problems of society and morality were in control. The average church member, living in such a non-hostile environment, saw little need to change his or her world. After all, Christian values were the norm. The relatively few problems were handled by those hired to do so. The clergy were our counselors, evangelists, mercy-givers, and teachers.

But the turmoil of the 1960s brought an end to this myth of utopia. The problems that had been internalized manifested themselves in a variety of acts of rebellion, immorality, and protest. "The moral hedges that surrounded our collective life have been trampled down," notes David Wells.[1] "What once was sublimated is now, in all of its raw and often violent nature, spewed forth in the name of liberty or self-expression. What once had to be private is now paraded publicly for the gallery of voyeurs. The virtues of the old privacy, such as reticence and modesty, are looked upon today as maladies. What was once unseemly is now commonplace," Wells laments.[2] He concludes, "In short, whereas once we were directed by a culture that had originally learned its habits from the Christian faith, we are now directed by a culture that has learned its habits from the psychologists."[3]

The American way of life is the envy of the world, but for most Americans happiness is elusive. In fact, as Wells notes, "The American version of happiness is quite lethal."[4] In 1991, more teenage boys died from gunshot wounds than from all natural causes combined. The United States has become a true world leader in the consumption of legal and illegal drugs. We also lead the world in divorce and in the incidence of depressive illnesses.[5] Our schools are symbols of chaos. No longer teaching values of right and wrong, Gerald Grant observes, "A teacher is less likely to insist that cheating is wrong than to ask why a cheater cheats."[6]

The decay of our society is a well-discussed issue. But in the midst of this dark cloud of bad news, our sovereign God has caused silver linings of hope to emerge. The good news is that the bad news has awakened Christians from their complacency. Admittedly the response to the self-destruction of society has not been limited to the church. Other groups with similar moral concerns are responding in increasing numbers. The church is leading the way in moral reformation.

Strangely, it may seem, it was the traditional church in the sixties and seventies that began to respond to the challenge of the decadent culture. Perhaps it was because the status quo was so upset that traditional-church members began to see the need for involvement. These believers also realized that the clergy alone could not do all that the church had to do. Ministry was imperative. Involvement was no longer optional.

The revolution of the lay ministry, like most revolutions, was a grassroots' movement. It did not begin with a few leaders deciding that a new program was in order. Instead it began with tens of thousands of laypersons from traditional churches seeking ways to be light in an ever-darkening world. Initially, some had to go outside the structure of their churches and join the ranks of parachurch organizations. But eventually the traditional churches, some of them at least, heard the message. They sought ways to equip their members to do the work of ministry (Eph. 4:11–12).

Before we proceed with further discussion of this revolution, we must understand its historical context. The lay ministry movement should have begun almost five centuries earlier. What happened then and what is happening now are closely related.

## The Reformation

Almost five hundred years ago, Martin Luther, John Calvin, and others began a revolution in the church. At that time, the clergy had a priestly role. Only they had the privilege to preside at the altar of the communion table as consecrated celebrants. Two levels of Christianity were present, and the common people were at the lower level.

Additionally, the leaders in the Roman Catholic hierarchy abused their positions. They took advantage of the people emotionally, spiritually, and financially. Greg Ogden notes,

> The stratified positions of status and honor were the seedbed for corruption during the Middle Ages as the church gained power equal to and often above the state. This dominance over people's lives was wedded to a theology that said Christ had delegated to the church

the right to dispense grace. Those in the hierarchy of the church therefore were in the powerful position of dispensing or withholding grace.[7]

Luther's statements were, therefore, nothing less than radical when he exclaimed, "Everyone who has been baptized may claim that he already has been consecrated a priest, bishop, or pope."[8] He further called for the priesthood of all believers when he said, "Let everyone, therefore, who knows himself to be a Christian be assured of this, and apply it to himself — that we are all priests, and there is no difference between us."[9]

The doctrine of justification by faith became central to the Reformation. The rediscovered gospel meant that any person is made right with God by their individual and personal response to the saving and forgiving grace of Jesus Christ. The church was not the dispenser of grace nor were the hierarchial leaders necessary for the people to relate to their Savior.

These rediscoveries of biblical truths had the potential to eliminate forever the wide chasm that existed between clergy and the laity. And, to be certain, from the sixteenth century until today the church has been immeasurably impacted by the work of the reformers. As Ogden notes, "According to the universal doctrine of the priesthood of all believers, as articulated by Luther, every Christian should be a minister of the Word of God."[10] Further says Ogden, "Luther's conviction that every believer is a mediator and intercessor between God and man had revolutionary potential for their conception of ministry."[11]

Protestantism was born out of the Reformation. Every non-Catholic believer today owes his or her heritage to the work of the brave individuals who risked much for the sake of biblical faith. Unfortunately, the clergy-laity bifurcation was never fully eliminated. David Watson observes,

> Most Protestant denominations have been as priest-ridden as the Roman Catholics. It is the minister, vicar, or pastor who has dominated the whole proceedings. Because of this heavy emphasis on clericalism, the laity have yet to fulfill their God-given call to ministry. In other words, the clergy-laity divisions have continued in much the same way as in pre-Reformation times, and the doctrine of spiritual gifts and body ministry have been largely ignored.[12]

In the Reformers' zeal to protect the rediscovered gospel, they soon established their own leadership structure in the churches. For most of the Reformed churches, the pastor was responsible for protecting the doctrine and carrying out the ordinances or administering the sacraments. Even the great Reformer John Calvin established an *Ecclesiastical Ordinance* which set forth four rigid offices in the church: pastors, teachers, elders, and deacons. His *Ordinance* was fully adopted by the Geneva city council.[13]

The sixteenth-century Reformation was a milestone in church history. It introduced believers to the biblical concept that all are priests through the High Priest, Jesus Christ (Heb. 7:26-28). Though the Reformation began a great new movement among the people in the church, it was incomplete. Because of the rigid ordering of the institutional church, the clergy-laity chasm was never fully bridged.

The traditional church in America is a direct descendant of the sixteenth-century Reformation church. The doctrine of the priesthood of believers is believed, taught, and proclaimed. But in reality many traditional churches are miles away from releasing all of their members for ministry. And no longer is structure prohibitive for ministry only because of clergy-laity chasm. New and imposing structures have been added which further bind the believer from following God's call to ministry within a local church. As one frustrated pastor shared with me—partly in jest, but mostly serious, "Jesus couldn't perform miracles in our church until the nominating committee had its monthly meeting and voted on Him for the new position of miracle worker."

Because the traditional church was so mired down in structure, and because so little ministry was done by the laity, a new reformation began to rise. It took the frustration of structure and the dire straits of society for this to grow, but it *is* growing. The new reformation has its roots in the traditional church, but its influence is spreading to all types of Christian churches across our land.

## The New Reformation[14]

"There is a fresh wind blowing in the church that is being felt wherever the doors are thrown open to include all of God's people in ministry," declares Ogden.[15] "We live in a day of a paradigm shift. We are on the verge of recapturing the biblical vision of the church as an organism in contrast to the church institution," Ogden further claims.[16] R. Paul Stevens writes, "It is not a day for one more program in lay training. It is a day for radical transformation of the whole people of God into a ministering people."[17] And Robert E. Slocum declares that the most important decision a church can make today is "the decision to shift the focus of your church from the ministry of the clergy to the ministry of the laity."[18] These relatively-recent proclamations reflect the sentiment of many who see a new era, a new reformation dawning in our churches.

We have previously discussed the incompleteness of the "first" Reformation. And we have seen factors that have encouraged a new reformation of unleashing the laity, particularly in traditional churches. Now we will examine the ways in which the new reformation is unfolding.

Many leaders have shared the vision of God's work among the laity in traditional churches. Lewis Drummond was among the first to see the relationship between the exercising of spiritual gifts by the laity and effective church evangelism.[19] C. Peter Wagner recognized a similar relationship between spiritual gift discovery and church growth.[20] But the late Ray Stedman was a key leader in this movement with his classic work, *Body Life*.[21]

Stedman illustrated the impact of Ephesians 4:11–12 upon lay ministry with the following diagram:[22]

**Figure 5.1: Ephesians 4:11–12**

The saints, all Christians, are equipped to do the work of ministry. This ministry in turn builds up the body. The ministry is not left in the hands of a few, but is the God-given responsibility of all the people of God.

For years the emphasis for church growth has been on dynamic leadership. It is certainly true that the church needs a pastor who is able to lead the people. Unfortunately, good leadership is often defined as omnicompetence. The pastor must be eloquent in the pulpit, scholarly in teaching, charming in person, evangelistic in relationships, compassionate to the hurting, organized in administration, and diligent in attendance of all church, denominational, civic, and social functions. Howard Snyder sees such a mindset as unhealthy: "If the pastor is a superstar, the church is an audience, not a body."[23]

Pastoral leadership, in its best and biblical role, is one that emphasizes the whole body rather than one person. The Holy Spirit is mentioned fifty-six times in Paul's letters; each passage refers to the Christian community rather than one individual.[24]

Perhaps one of the most recognized churches in the new reformation is Bear Valley Baptist Church in Denver, Colorado. This church became a symbol for the laity-ministry movement when Frank Tillapuagh, then the senior pastor, wrote a book about the revolution in his traditional church. *Unleashing the Church*, published in 1982, became a manual for churches desiring to break out of their organizational ruts.[25]

When Tillapuagh first came to Bear Valley there were over twenty committees in the church. "Fortunately," the pastor commented, "there weren't enough people to fill them so they were all nonfunctional."[26] Since then changes have been impressive. In 1970, the church had 100 active members; ten years later that number was over 1000. In the same period the budget increased from $16,000 to over $500,000. But even more impressive than the numerical growth has been the number of people involved in ministries and the depth of their commitment.

Bear Valley and other traditional churches that are truly "unleashed" have applied biblical strategy in various ways. Yet I have discovered the following five common elements.

### The Pastor Is a Servant Leader

He does not seek to have the spotlight shining on him at all times. He rejoices when others get the credit for ministries. He trusts the people of his church to do the work of ministry and sees his role as primarily that of an equipper. He shares the pastoral responsibilities with other paid staff or unpaid laypersons.

### The Ministry of the Laity Is an Ongoing Theme

When the pastor is in the pulpit, he often mentions the ministries in the church. The church bulletin or newsletter highlights them. In the worship service, testimonies by laypersons about their ministry involvement is common. An annual banquet or ministry display, is also held to celebrate God's work through the people.

## Spiritual Gifts Are Emphasized

Through an established method, people are taught about the biblical concept of spiritual gifts. It includes means by which believers can discover their own spiritual gifts. One or more persons are responsible for accumulating and maintaining information on giftedness and desires for ministry. No person is presented a ministry opportunity without first considering his or her own spiritual gift mix.

## The People Are Given "Permission" to Do Ministry

The leadership of the church encourages people to be involved in ministries or to create new ministries where none exist. Church leaders communicate trust in the people and, more importantly, in the Holy Spirit to lead them into new ministries.

## The Vision of the Church Reflects the Spiritual Gifts and Ministries of the People

The church's vision is clear and communicated often. It is not unilaterally dictated by a singular leader. Instead the vision flows naturally from the way God is using people of the church in ministry.

## The Pastor in the New Reformation

Elton Trueblood, writing in the early years of the new reformation, describes the pastor as one "who possess(es) the peculiar gift of being able to help other men and women to practice any ministry to which they are called."[27] A key purpose of the pastor is to give away ministry.

The Greek word *katartismos* (Eph. 4:12) is translated in various ways: "equip" in the Revised Standard Version, "perfect" in the King James Version, and "prepare" in the New International Version.[28] Basically it can be defined in three ways.

First, "equip" means "to mend or to restore." In Galatians 6:1, Paul admonishes the church to "restore" the person caught in sin. The essence of restoration is to fix that which is broken. The pastor's ministry, then is one of correcting that which is not as it should be. This ministry can be doctrinal in nature or it can mean providing the leadership needed to bring the church in line with God's plan for her. Or it can involve restoration of fallen sinners as Paul exhorts in 2 Corinthians 2:5–11. In any case, "equip" is a leadership function which is corrective and restorative in nature.

A second definition of "equip" is "to establish or to lay foundations." Along with the foundation of Jesus Christ, the written Word of God is necessary to build Christ's church. When Paul wrote to Timothy, he explicitly said that Scripture has an equipping element in it: "All Scripture is God-breathed and is useful. . . in righteousness, so that the man of God may be thoroughly *equipped* for every good work" (2 Tim. 3:16–17 emphasis added). When the pastor teaches and preaches, his words not only instruct and inform believers, they equip them for ministry as well.

A third understanding of "equip" is "to prepare or train." Ogden comments, "If it is true that all ministry is body ministry, then every area traditionally associated with pastoral ministry—with the possible exception of preaching—can be performed by duly gifted and called members of the body."[29] What then does the pastor do? Ogden further notes, "The pastor's role, therefore is not to do the body's ministry, but to build teams of people to share the ministry in the different aspects of the pastor's giftedness."[30]

In the traditional church in America, it is unlikely that the pastor will announce that he will cease doing all ministry except equipping, and that he expects the people to do it instead. Such a pastor's tenure would not survive the next business meeting. Many of our traditional church members are unprepared for such radical change. They are like the characters in a cartoon who make up a pastor search committee. The obvious chairperson of the committee addresses the prospective pastor with these words: "We see our pastor as one who primarily administrates, enables, coordinates . . . and scrapes the pigeon droppings off the steeple."

Wise leaders in traditional churches are slowly and methodically educating and training their people to do ministry. In my previous book, *Eating the Elephant,* I compared the leadership of a traditional church to the task of eating an elephant. It can only be done one bite (step) at a time. But it can be done. Traditional churches are unleashing their people to do ministry. Pastors have been able to see this new power for ministry unharnessed through the unbelievable phenomenon of spiritual gifts discovery.

## The Spiritual Gift Phenomenon

It is difficult to decide what is more amazing. With all the emphasis on spiritual gifts in the Bible, it is amazing that the doctrine has been neglected for so many centuries. But it is equally amazing to witness the explosion of spiritual gift awareness over the past three decades. Larry Gilbert, president of Church Growth Institute, says that their spiritual gift inventories have been one of their most-consistent, best-selling products.[31] The simple inventory asks a series of questions about a person's inclinations in certain situations. The inventory is then "scored" and gift mixes are suggested by the score.

We offered a spiritual gift seminar in a church I pastored. It ended with each participant answering the inventory questions. We then scheduled individual appointments with a member of the pastoral team.

A retired woman was the first to discuss her spiritual gift inventory results with me. She had returned to the church after almost two decades of absence and she was very enthusiastic about getting back into church life. She had willingly accepted our offer for her to teach fourth graders in Sunday School and she had been teaching for six months when she took the inventory.

When I shared her spiritual gift mix depicted on the inventory, it showed that one of the last things she should do is teach children. "Oh," she exclaimed. "That's why I've been so miserable teaching that class! And I felt guilty for being miserable!"

Because her dominant gift was administration, I suggested that she try volunteer work in the church office, which was desperately needed. She agreed to work ten hours a week, and contributed wonderfully in this ministry. She also experienced the joy of doing what God had gifted and called her to do.

Though I have used the adjective "amazing" several times, I must mention how amazing it is the spiritual gift phenomenon has received so little notice. Until recent years, 1 Corinthians 12–14 has been little more than theory for most Christians. And the "love chapter," 1 Corinthians 13, was hardly recognized as the foundation for utilizing spiritual gifts. I agree heartily with Greg Ogden who predicts that "we live in the generation when the unfinished business of the Reformation may at last be completed."[32]

The implications of the rediscovery of the ministry of the laity through the rediscovery of spiritual gifts are staggering. In tens of thousands of churches across America and beyond, millions of Christians are discovering their spiritual gifts for use in ministry. An army of unfathomable size will be doing ministry at a level not unlike that of the early church in Jerusalem. And like that early church, the new mobilization of believers will result in thousands being drawn to the Savior.

## Lay Ministry and Church Growth

When Kirk Hadaway conducted a study of factors which engender church growth, he found two issues closely associated with lay ministry. First, the stronger the lay leadership in a church, the greater the likelihood is for numerical growth.[33] This correlation was particularly strong for larger churches, but the relationship between lay leadership and growth was apparent in smaller churches as well.

The strongest correlation, however, was between a church's willingness to change and church growth.[34] A receptivity to necessary changes was a key in those churches that were once plateaued or declining, but now are experiencing growth.

Such a correlation can be easily understood if a church is to make the necessary changes to unleash the laity for ministry. The people of the church must reject the idea that all of their programs and ministries are an end unto themselves. They must be open to new and challenging ministries that may test their spiritual character. They must forever abandon their unspoken motto of "We've never done it that way before."

Now it may seem that I am suggesting that a traditional church should forsake its traditions for something new and unknown. To the contrary, I believe the church should reclaim its traditions rather than abandon them. However, true traditions are not the ministries or committees that have little relevance other than giving members something to do. No, the true traditions are the motives and desires that gave birth originally to these functions. They were created to address a need at the time of their inception. Like the founding members and others who were open to new ministries in order to reach people in their communities, so should the churchgoers of today be open to ministries that address contemporary needs.

## The Laity in the Twenty-first Century Traditional Church

Since the new reformation has its seeds in the traditional church, what will be the role of the laity in the twenty-first century traditional church? It would appear that the involved church member of the twenty-first century will have five noticeable characteristics.

## Better Appreciation of Church Membership

For many churches, membership means little or nothing. This is quite a contrast to the churches of the first few centuries when identification with the church meant taking the cross of Christ, even to martyrdom.[35]

Slowly traditional churches are rethinking their concepts of church membership. More and more churches are raising their expectation levels for their members. And as the expectation levels are raised, the members become more appreciative of what it means to be a part of the body of Christ.

Of course this will cause some members to drop out of the church. While we should do everything possible to retain and reclaim these people, we must ultimately understand that many are unwilling to pay the price of commitment. These church members may need evangelizing more than assimilating.

The members who remain will comprise a much stronger church. Inactive rolls will decline and a new sense of unity and purpose will draw the believers closer together.

## Better-Equipped Laity

Since greater numbers of church members are doing the work of ministry, church leaders take on the primary role of equipping. Numerous resources are now available to assist the pastor and other church leaders to equip the people for ministry.

In the first chapter we discussed the great prayer movement that is sweeping our nation. Nell Bruce is minister of prayer at Highview Baptist Church in Louisville, Kentucky, where Bill Hancock is the pastor. Many churches are calling her to come teach their members to pray, and she is not the only equipper for prayer ministries that has shared this trend with me. If our people in traditional churches become equipped as Spirit-empowered prayer warriors, the possibilities for God's miraculous works in our nation are unlimited.

## Creators of New Ministries

The laypeople of the twenty-first century traditional church will not only become involved in existing ministries and programs in their churches, they will have the freedom to begin new ministries as God leads them. Can you imagine the explosion of new ministries that will be started? No longer will the creation of a ministry be limited to denominational and local church leaders; it will be the domain of all God's people.

## Supporters of Pastor and Other Staff

In many churches great tension exists between the pastor and some of the people. Much has been written about pastoral termination and pastoral burnout over the past few years. At least one reason for this tension is that the average church member has no concept about the demands of ministry.

However, when the laity of the church starts doing more of the ministry work, they will take a significant load off the pastor and staff. Burnout will be significantly reduced. More importantly, the laity will better understand the ministry the pastor provides. Involved laypersons involved are less likely to be critical of the leadership.

## Participants in a New Evangelistic Harvest

Imagine this scenario: First Baptist Church averages 185 in attendance, but its total membership is 255. The great majority of the members are in attendance on a given Sunday—not a typical traditional church.

Of the 193 adults, over 150 have been equipped for different ministries. Over twenty adults are involved in intentional evangelistic ministries. Fifteen members consistently visit hospitals and the homebound each week. Almost one-third of the adults are involved in a variety of teaching ministries. And nearly forty-five members give of their time weekly to eight different ministries the church started in order to reach the community for Christ.

Though the geographic community is small and declining slightly, not a week goes by that at least two or three people are reached for Christ. Some are baptized and remain in the church; others are transient and move on. But they are all touched by the Savior through First Baptist.

A year ago the church had 145 in average attendance. All the recent growth is due to conversions and baptisms. The little church in the little town is making a big difference for the Kingdom. And it will continue to do so in the years ahead.

I am not a prophet, but I see similar evangelistic harvests taking place in traditional churches across our land in the years ahead. As more and more believers in the church are unleashed and equipped for ministry, the unbelieving world will see that we are not only different, but we are making a difference. These unbelievers may recognize that we have something they do not—joy, peace, and love.

Then they too will be drawn to the church where they will meet the Savior for whom we do ministry—for His glory and honor.

# Chapter 6

# "Above Reproach . . ."
# Church Trend 6:
# The New Traditional Church Pastor

It is true that matters of spirituality loom large in the churches, but it is not at all clear that churches expect the pastor to do anything more than to be a good friend. The older role of the pastor as broker of truth has been eclipsed by the newer managerial functions.

—David F. Wells

THE GENTLE CRASHING OF THE SMALL waves provide a calm serenity that John Cruden has not experienced in a decade. But he knows that the moments of peace and tranquility are temporary. This retreat to a borrowed condominium on the white sands of the Gulf of Mexico will end in four days. Then the worn-down, burned-out pastor must come to grips with several major decisions.

In his twenty years of pastoral ministry, John has seen the expectations and demands upon the pastorate change dramatically. *Dramatically*, the pastor reflects. *That's an understatement. More like revolutionary.* And on this warm summer night, the pastor lies awake in his bed as the clock hands slip past midnight. His bride of twenty-four years sleeps softly. *What would I have done without her?* he ponders. And then he says a brief prayer of thanksgiving to God for the woman he loves so deeply. With the help of God and his wife, John knows he will make it. He is not sure just how, but he knows.

John Cruden remembers those challenging days at seminary. Greek. Hebrew. New Testament. Old Testament. Church History. Theology . . . and on and on. But the demands of study and the rigors of the classroom did not deter him because he was certain of his call from God. His days at seminary were to be used to build the theological foundation from which he would communicate God's truths to equip the believers for life and ministry.

But even as he left seminary to accept his first full-time pastorate, the winds of change were blowing. John did not notice the subtle changes at first. Later they would be unmistakably obvious.

*My first two years in the pastorate were days of continued study in God's Word,* he reflects. He performed his pastoral duties such as visiting, weddings, and funerals, but the larger segments of his time were spent in study so that he could better equip his church members. Shortly thereafter his schedule changed. *My counseling demands really began to increase in that third year,* he remembers. Perhaps that was the beginning of the problems.

As the years went by, John became more involved in tasks for which he had no real training and, in many cases, little desire to do. He read some of the many books on leadership and management, and he eagerly desired to be a better church leader. But he never expected his continuing education in leadership to be so time consuming.

He experienced the same level of frustration trying to keep up with the latest church growth methodologies. His time was consumed by things that, in years past, had not existed. And much to his chagrin, the areas of his pastoral ministry which were suffering the most were his personal prayer time and Bible study. How could he feed his flock when he was malnourished himself?

Equally frustrating to John were the new expectations of the church members. Although much had always been expected of pastors, now he was expected to be an astute leader, manager, and CEO. Were these added responsibilities really part of God's call in his life?

And so, on that warm July evening, John Cruden opens the window to hear more clearly the steady and calming sound of the gulf waves. *God is sovereign,* John reminds himself. *He has my life in His hands.* And then a prayer arises from the depths of his heart: *Dear God, I'm tired and confused. You called me. You will not forsake me. Please show me clearly the next step. I place my trust in You alone.*

## Pastors Adrift

The exponential increase in forced pastoral terminations and the number of pastors leaving the ministry due to burnout is a recent manifestation of a problem that has been growing for decades. In fact some mark the middle of the eighteenth century as the point where the Christian minister began to decline in public perception.[1] David Wells notes that since 1850, "ministers were increasingly depicted in fiction as either irrelevant or worthy of derision."[2] The fallen clergy included Nathaniel Hawthorne's Arthur Dimmesdale, Sinclair Lewis's Elmer Ganty, and Peter DeVrie's Andrew Mackerel.[3] Though the public esteem of the clergy was slipping in some quarters, the typical minister was unaffected by the caricatures. He was, particularly in the community in which he served, still a person of prominence and respect.

However, the length of time a pastor served a community began to decrease around the middle of the nineteenth century; pastors were becoming more mobile. Prior to the nineteenth century, the strong bond between pastor and church and between pastor and community was partly due to pastoral longevity. For example, 221 ministerial students graduated from Yale College between 1745 and 1755. An astounding 71 percent of these men remained in their first pastorate until their deaths. And only 4 percent had four or more pastorates.[4]

Today the average pastoral tenure is between two and three years. Though this time is short, it is by no means a recent phenomenon. In 1800, the average pastoral tenure in a Presbyterian or Congregationalist church in New Hampshire was twenty years. By 1810, just one decade later, the number had fallen to fifteen years. In 1830, the average tenure was only five years; thirty years later in 1860 the number was less then four years, a number which has remained fairly stable for over 130 years.[5]

For most churches in the nineteenth century, permanence was an important issue. Churches would often cling to their pastors despite inept preaching, poor evangelistic results, or dubious interpersonal skills. The local minister was an important part of the community fabric and his departure disrupted not only the church, but the entire town. Stability was important — vitally important.

Many theorists speculate that the mobile American society provides a good explanation for the modern mobile pastor. After all, they argue, a pastor of a suburban church in a growth area may see one-fourth of his flock move in and out of the church in one year. Of what benefit is a long-term pastorate if the membership has a turnover every five years or so?

This argument is based on at least two fallacies. First, the American pastor became mobile long before the nation at large began its adventure into destabilization. As noted previously, the short tenure of pastors is a trend that is almost two centuries old. The second fallacy is that a church with highly-mobile members will not benefit from a long-term (dare we suggest lifetime?) pastorate. To the contrary, the stability offered by a pastor with long tenure is of *greater* need in these churches.

As I argued in a previous book,[6] an established church needs a pastor to lead the church through incremental change and growth. Sudden and massive changes often do more harm than good. Although long-term pastorates do not guarantee growth or provide assurance that a church will be in God's will, a series of short-term pastorates inevitably mean that disruption and discontinuity will be the norm.

Prior to the nineteenth century the relationship between the pastor and his church was covenantal in nature. The compact between the two parties had at least some similarities to the marriage agreement. Breaking the ties between church and pastor was a long and arduous process. If a minister made a move from one church to another, he would often be required to get the consent of the original church and all of the surrounding churches in the area.[7]

These lifetime ministerial expectations were vitally important, even if the pastor moved to another church before his death. This pattern of ministry offered the church stability built upon trust. Motives were rarely questioned because the members knew that their pastor had to endure the consequences of his actions with them. Contrast this with the atitude of a deacon in a church I pastored. The nagging deacon would question every leadership decision I made with the comment, "Pastor, we'll have to live with your decisions long after you've gone!" (He was right!)

Long-term or lifetime ministries also meant freedom for the pastor. He could make long-term decisions instead of quick-fix solutions. He did not have to jump at every new methodology that came his way. More importantly, he had security. This security meant that he could preach the whole counsel of God without fear of retribution or dismissal.

What then caused this shift to shorter-term pastorates? Unfortunately, most of the blame then and today lies with the pastors. In the nineteenth century, when hints of declining pastoral respect were implicit in literature, pastors began to seek respect in other ways. Instead of being secure and confident in their own personal sense of calling, they sought the prestige of other professions, such as law and medicine. This prestige, in a secular sense, could not be earned by being the pastor of one small church for a lifetime. It meant that upward mobility (i.e. bigger churches) was a necessity for "real" advancement.

David Wells comments on this sad scenario: "The notion that one's occupation might serve as the means to provide a career was quite foreign at the beginning of the nineteenth century but quite common by its end."[8] Wells laments the implications of this change: "Having a career came to mean making progress, moving from preparatory stages of accomplishment up the ladder to larger honor and responsibilities. The occupation in which one was engaged was no longer an end in itself but the means to an end—specifically, the elevation or enrichment of the worker."[9]

Many pastors forsook the path of servanthood for the fleeting praises of those men and women who are dubiously impressed with larger churches. But this experiment backfired; it increased the pressures and demands on the pastor. For it is he who told the church members the criteria for a successful pastorate—a higher rung on the career ladder. Because the pastor placed himself on a secular model of success, many church members now hold him accountable to that model. And if he fails, he is gone.

David Wells again expresses the situation cogently: "These changes also echoed rather ominously through the ministry. For if it is the case that careers can be had in the church, then it is inevitable that ministers will be judged by the height to which they ascend on the ladder of achievement, and they in turn will judge the church on the extent to which it facilitates this ascend."[10] This model is not the biblical model of servant leadership personified by the Savior. Wells comments that it is difficult to comprehend "how such calculations can be reconciled with the biblical notion of service, the call to serve the church without thought of what one might receive in return."[11]

The moral failure of many pastors and the televangelists' scandals are responsible for the decline of pastoral respect in America. Those incidents are merely symptomatic of a longer, deeper problem. Some pastors have forsaken the God of Scripture for the god of self. In doing so, they have not only broken trust with God, they have also broken trust with God's people. So when they do finally fall, no one offers a hand of redemption and restoration. There is neither bond nor trust. What was once unthinkable in an earlier time—the moral failure of a called man of God—has become commonplace and, more tragically, accepted.

## Recent Pastoral Models

In many seminary catalogs and church conference advertisements the phrase "biblically relevant" is used rather loosely. For some pastors those two words are a cruel oxymoron, an ideal impossible to achieve. Many feel that one must choose between being biblical and being relevant. Or stated another way, one must decide if he or she is willing to forsake the evangelization of postmodernity in order to be biblically faithful. As one pastor of a large and growing church once told me, "We try not to say much about theology around here. It would just confuse the folks we're trying to reach."

But I see a new and encouraging trend emerging. It is a trend which means that the pastor can be both biblical and relevant. And this new direction is directly related to other movements previously addressed, particularly prayer and biblical faithfulness.

Before we look specifically at this emerging trend, let us place it in a proper historical and contemporary context. In the earliest times of the Roman Catholic Church, the priestly role dominated the clerical role. Priests were seen as mediators between God and humanity as they offered Christ in the Eucharist. All other pastoral rules were peripheral to this central function.

Earlier we mentioned the Reformation and the impact it had upon the church, particularly from the laity's point of view. The Reformation also shifted the role of the pastor. Although ministers still fulfilled their roles of teaching, praying, administering the sacraments, caring for the needy, and leading the church, preaching the message of salvation was central. The message of God's forgiveness and grace, and faith in the Lord Jesus Christ could not be silenced. Freed from the shackles of ecclesiastical salvation, these new Protestant preachers proclaimed their messages with fervency and urgency. Pastors often preached seven or more times each week, covering several different areas of the Bible.[12]

The Puritan, Richard Baxter, was a tremendous influence on succeeding generations of pastors. Baxter clearly understood the pastoral role: "The first and main point I submit to you is that it is the unquestionable duty of all ministers of the Church to catechize and to teach personally all who are submitted to their care."[13] In our contemporary understanding, Baxter's emphasis would be called personal discipling, with a heavy emphasis upon equipping, evangelizing, and thorough biblical teaching.

The contrast between today's generation of pastors and those of yesteryear is stark when one looks at roles and expectations. In the beginning of this chapter we met John Cruden. He faced burnout and dropout because he lacked certitude about his role in ministry. Forces pulled him in so many directions that he was figuratively falling apart. This uncertainty weakens the church as well. James E. Means notes that, "while no definitive new conception of pastoral ministry has emerged, uncertainty about pastoral authority, vagueness about priorities, and a confusion of subroles with a pastor's primary role continue to weaken the church."[14]

New and varied expectations have complicated the pastoral role in recent years. Some of these new responsibilities are far from the biblically defined role of the pastor.

### The Omnicompetent Pastor

While pastoring a large church in Birmingham, I was asked by one of the members to resolve a brewing problem in the kitchen and fellowship hall. We had recently built a facility that was one of the largest and most modern of its kind. Although I cannot recall the nature of the problem, I do remember that two sides were in opposition to one another. Because the issue was over some aspect of the kitchen, I was totally at a loss to make a decision or bring unity to the schism.

I finally admitted to one of the quarreling parties that I could not solve the problem. Her response is forever etched in my memory: "And you call yourself a pastor!" I guess I must now add Kitchens and Fellowship Halls 101 to my seminary's curriculum!

Not only are expectations high for the pastor, but there are so many of them. I recently gave the deacons of a church I pastored in St. Petersburg, Florida, a survey to complete. I asked them to write, in number of hours, what their minimum expectations of me were. If I satisfied every deacon's minimum expectations, my work week would be as follows:

> Prayer—14 hours
> Sermon preparation—18 hours
> Outreach visitation—10 hours
> Counseling—10 hours
> Hospital and home visitation—15 hours
> Administrative functions—18 hours
> Community involvement—5 hours
> Denominational involvement—5 hours
> Church meetings—5 hours
> Worship services/preaching—10 hours

Other—4 hours
TOTAL—114 hours per week

So much for sleeping! While some pastors do put pressure upon themselves, the demands from within the church are significant. Means notes that "congregational dissatisfaction with pastors who produce poor statistics manifests itself with appalling frequency. Pastoral firings and forced resignations have dramatically increased in the last ten years, approaching ten percent annually in some denominations. The number of battered pastors is a scandal of the American church. In other times, pastors could expect persecution from the world; now mistreatment is more likely to come from within the church."[15]

### The Dependency-Creating Pastor

In the previous chapter we examined a great movement of God that is resulting in millions of laypeople released to do the work of ministry. Yet these people have to be in churches where their pastors create a sense of freedom rather than dependency.

Unfortunately, some pastors still follow the model of making the church dependent on them. Oftentimes this dependency plays itself out in counseling sessions. Counseling can quickly become the most time-consuming activity on the daily calendar. While we cannot deny the need for counseling, most pastors are neither equipped nor called for this type of ministry. Pastoral concern and listening skills are imperative but long-term and extensive counseling can be dangerous. Many pastors who have succumbed to moral failure testify that the temptation began in counseling sessions.

A pastor can suspect a dependent mindset when he hears the words, "After all, that's what we pay him for." The church member believes that by virtue of his or her tithe or offering, the pastor must function at his or her request. Rarely, if ever, are dependent church members content. They typically have a cynical view of their pastor as indicated in this satirical letter:

Dear Church Member:
This chain letter is meant to bring happiness to you. Unlike other chain letters, it does not cost money. Simply send a copy of this letter to six other churches who are tired of their pastors. Then bundle up your pastor and send him to the church at the bottom of the list. In one week you will receive 16,436 pastors

and one of them should be a dandy! Have faith in this letter. One church broke the chain and got their old pastor back.[16]

Contented and fulfilled church members are those who see their ministries as part of God's plan for the church. They view their pastors as equippers rather than ubiquitous supermen. Malcontents are dependent upon pastors. And they are the type of church members who may stuff their pastors in a chain letter.

## The CEO

A strong positive correlation exists between capable pastoral leadership and evangelistic growth in a church. C. Kirk Hadaway observes: "Even though autocratic, commander-style leadership seems unrelated to church growth, if can be said that the pastors of growing churches tend to be *strong* leaders."[17] Hadaway's conclusions were the result of a study which showed "that in growing churches 63 percent of the pastors say they view their role as that of a quarterback . . . as compared to 46 percent of plateaued church pastors and 32 percent of declining church pastors. The majority of nongrowing church pastors say they are either facilitators or 'hired hands.'"[18]

The Church Growth Movement has flooded Christian churches with leadership books, videos, and conferences. Leadership has been advocated repeatedly as a leading church growth principle, if not the first principle. Indeed I have given a prominent role to the leadership principle in my own writings.[19]

Church growth leaders acknowledge basic observations when they make claims to the high correlation between strong pastoral leadership and evangelistic church growth. And few Christians want to be involved in ministry or belong to a church where the pastor is a weak or incapable leader. A danger exists, however, when this principle is given such a high profile. One may get the impression that a pastor only needs certain leadership skills and managerial training to be perfectly equipped for the job.

The pastor may then see himself a chief executive officer (CEO) whose key functions include the managerial tasks of a business. Now this view has never been advocated by the leadership of the Church Growth Movement, but some pastors have heard only a part of the message. The church ultimately suffers when its pastor is first a manager, and secondly an equipper, a pray-er, a studier of the Word, and a preacher. Leadership skills are vitally important. But the pastor must first be a man of the Word; being a CEO is not in his biblical "job description."

### The Competitor

Means notes that too many pastors see themselves and their churches as competitors.[20] Numerical growth or decline becomes a barometer by which the pastor's success or failure is measured. "In other words, the pastoral role that formerly centered on preaching-teaching, care giving, and equipping has become one focused on rivalry with other pastors and churches, with thriving organizations as the prize for competing successfully," says Means.[21] How is success determined? Means continues, "Success or failure in pastoral ministry reveals itself in superior physical facilities, bigger budgets, more attractive programming, and fuller pews than other churches in town. In order to compete successfully, churches become reflectors of community culture not the molders of it."[22]

What all distortions of the pastoral role have in common is the problem of emphasizing other aspects of ministry to the neglect of the biblical model of the pastor. Numbers are important, for example. They engender accountability and represent people. Those who toss verbal potshots at numerical emphases fail to realize the positive benefits of counting. Biblically, counting can be from God (2 Sam. 24:1) or from Satan (1 Chron. 21:1).

The same can be said of pastoral counseling. The pastor should counsel the people of his church. However, when that activity takes place to the detriment of prayer, equipping, preaching, or Bible study, it has become a distortion of the pastoral role.

The encouraging trend is that pastors are returning to a biblical model. Once again we are seeing a movement back to a more traditional model. Let us look briefly at the implications of this trend.

### John Cruden and the Acts 6 Model

We now return to the story of Pastor John Cruden, our noble but hurting character. In the middle of his sleepless night, he begins to read his Bible. John finds himself in Acts 6 where the Grecian Jews were complaining against the Hebraic Jews because their widows were not receiving their daily distribution of food. *Typical church,* John says to himself. *People fighting because they are not getting their way.*

Then his eyes move further down the text. He has read these words a hundred times, but now they almost jump off the page. "So the Twelve gathered all the disciples together and said, 'It would not be right for us to neglect the ministry of the word of God in order to wait on tables . . . . We . . . will give our attention to prayer and the ministry of the word'" (Acts 6:2, 4).

Before tonight John saw these words as an explanation for the deacon ministry. Now he sees an additional meaning. *Those apostles had ministry demands coming from all directions, he thinks. But they still insisted that they would not get distracted; prayer and the Word would remain their focus.*

John Cruden is tempted to awaken his wife and share this clear message from God. Instead, he walks to the balcony and breathes in the fresh salt-water air. And he says a prayer of gratitude to the sovereign God who promised He would never leave or forsake him.

## The Acts 6 Revolution Among Pastors

The revolutions mentioned in earlier chapters have touched both laity and pastors alike. But for the pastor this revolution will mean a significant shift from contemporary models of ministry. The trend is for the twenty-first century pastor to do ministry more like the first-century pastor. Church growth methodologies, counseling, leadership training, and other areas will be important, but the bulk of the pastor's time will be spent like the apostles of Acts 6 in prayer and ministry of the Word.

### Praying Pastors

In my final weeks as pastor of Green Valley Baptist Church, we had a prayer conference led by Don Miller. I found myself wishing at times that Don had come into my life at an earlier point in my ministry. Though I knew that prayer was important, that conference reminded me that prayer was not just another ministry for me, it was the lifeline to everything I did for the kingdom. And God graciously reminded me that this focus would be something I could communicate to seminary students for generations to come as a seminary dean and professor.

The great prayer movement celebrated in chapter 1 is not just affecting church laypeople. It is touching the lives of pastors in ways that will reshape the concept of pastoral ministry in the next century. A new generation of prayer warriors is rising up to lead churches in the twenty-first century.

## Bible-Hungry Pastors

I believe "hunger" is a good metaphor to describe the attitude of a growing number of pastors toward God's Word. In chapter 2 we saw a rediscovery of theology and the Bible taking place in churches. Pastors will be among the many who will devote literally hours a day to the study of the Word.

The description of the pastor in Ephesians 4:11–12 is essentially the double phrase "pastor-teacher." The pastor's task is inherent in the title. Pastors are to teach and preach the content of the Christian faith. They are to feed the flock of God (1 Pet. 5:2). William Barclay says, "The shepherd of the flock of God is the man who bears God's people on his heart, who feeds them with the truth, who seeks them when they stray away, and who defends them from all that would hurt or destroy of distort their faith."[23] How vitally important it becomes, then, for the pastor to be grounded and well-studied in God's Word.

We have almost passed through a phase where relevance has been the guiding force of the pastoral ministry. I use the word "almost" because many pastors are still in this paradigm. Since postmodernity is such a peculiar culture with no clear marks except the rejection of modernity as truth, churches here experienced great difficulties understanding this culture. Yet they honestly desire to reach the people who comprise the culture. A key concept in the late eighties and early nineties, therefore, became "relevance." How can we be relevant to a society that largely views the church as irrelevant?

However, in their enthusiasm to reach the culture, relevance became paramount, and biblical truths became secondary. These churches did not consciously reject God's Word; they simply had higher priorities.

The pastors of these churches spent large amounts of time attending conferences about the most current methodologies; reading books that dealt with similar issues; and designing ministries and programs that would be user-friendly or relevant to contemporary society. They were not wrong in doing so; but other disciplines suffered as more time was consumed by these activities.

A slow but perceptible shift is underway. The Bible is returning as the key "church growth manual." Pastors are waking up to the fact that long-term, sustained growth can only take place when the people are nurtured, taught, and educated in God's work. The pastor, therefore, must be biblically equipped himself.

In the twenty-first century, pastors will spend more of their time in "the ministry of the Word." When they do attend conferences or meet informally with peers, the focus will be upon ageless biblical issues rather than the latest methodological fad.

And as the pastor immerses himself more in the Word he, in turn, is discipling and equipping the church for ministry. The greatest church growth "tool" has been right in our hands all along.

## Equipping Pastors

Since we discussed the equipping pastor in detail in the previous chapter (see "The Pastor in the New Reformation"), we will not spend much time here. Yet one additional point is noteworthy.

The Acts 6 model of the apostolic ministry essentially moves the pastor to the ministries of prayer and the Word. When we come to Ephesians 4:12 and see the role of the pastor-teacher to be an equipper, we must see this role in light of the Acts 6 model.

The equipping pastor is one who obediently works within the mandate to do the ministry of the Word. The clearest New Testament equippers were those who preached and taught God's Word with conviction. Preaching is not simply one item of a lengthy pastoral job description; it is a key component of the equipping ministry. Teaching, too, would be a key equipping function. Even the Puritan pastor Richard Baxter, whose passion was individual discipleship, saw his primary role to be a teaching equipper.

In essence then, the Acts 6 model for pastoral ministry is complete in its brevity. Prayer and the ministry of the Word are the sum and substance of the pastoral role. And within the purview of the ministry of the Word is the vitally important task of equipping others to do the work of ministry.

## Models of Integrity

When the pastor intended to stay at one church for a lifetime, violations of moral and ethical issues were rare. The high positive correlation between long pastoral tenure and ethical responsibility was not coincidental. When a pastor knew that he would live in the same community and minister to the same families for decades, he could not run easily from moral problems he created.

On a more positive note, the long-term pastorates engendered greater accountability. The longer a pastor was among the same people, the greater was the likelihood for both formal and informal systems of accountability.

The lifetime view of the pastorate freed the pastor from emulating the secular world where ladder climbing was and is the norm. The pastor of the smallest church was held in the same respect and esteem as his counterparts in larger churches. The mere fact that one had been called to pastoral ministry by the living God was all that was needed for ego fulfillment.

The fall of so many ministers, particularly television ministers, should not have shocked us. For decades the pastoral ministry had become more blended with culture. It is little surprise then that secular moral values (or lack of values) became those of the ministry.

Thankfully, a new day is emerging in pastoral ministry. Because pastors are spending more time in prayer and the Word, they are taking on *His* values and *His* morals. Will it not be a joyous day when the pastoral role is seen as the human paradigm for virtue and morality?

The secular world is ready for this moral leadership. They know such leaders will not be found in politics, business, entertainment, or sports. When Stephen R. Covey wrote *The Seven Habits of Highly Effective People*[24] in 1989, the book became an instant bestseller. The promotional leads for the book used such words as "fairness," "integrity," "honesty," and "human dignity." A great hunger for moral leadership principles was evident as the book continued to be a top seller over the next few years.

Yet American morality was not changed by Covey's book. Though his principles were sound, Covey was not writing as a believer in Jesus Christ. He did not tell the world about the one true Power to become a person of fairness, integrity, honesty, and dignity. He told the world how they *should* be; but he did not tell them that their situation was hopeless without a personal relationship with Christ.

The good news is that many pastors in the twenty-first century will become models of integrity. Such is not to say that pastors will be viewed as saints of perfection. But many will be leaders in their communities because of their very character.

One of the most humbling honors of my life was to become the founding dean of the Billy Graham School of Missions, Evangelism, and Church Growth at The Southern Baptist Theological Seminary. I was grateful to be a part of something to which Billy Graham gave his name.

Our president, R. Albert Mohler, told me about the day he asked Dr. Graham if he would give his name to the school. The great evangelist's initial response was to decline. He felt unworthy of the honor. That attitude of humility is one of the reasons Billy Graham has been used of God is such miraculous ways. In the years ahead, as ministers devote themselves increasingly to prayer and God's Word, the world will have thousands of Christlike models. Paul's plea to the Roman Christians will be heeded by many: "Therefore, I urge you, brothers, in view of God's mercy, to offer your bodies as living sacrifices, holy and pleasing to God—which is your spiritual worship. Do not conform any longer to the pattern of this world, but be transformed by the renewing of your mind. Then you will be able to test and approve what God's will is—his good, pleasing, and perfect will" (Rom. 12:1–2).

## Covenantal Relationships

The covenants between God and His people are central themes in the Bible. Noah received the first covenant (Gen. 9:9–17) when God promised not to repeat the flood. God's second biblical covenant was with Abraham (Gen. 15:18; 17:2). The divine promise meant that Abraham's descendants would take and occupy the land of Canaan, which thus became known as "the promised land."

The covenant of Jesus became the New Testament. Jesus used the Last Supper to interpret His ministry and death. His sacrifice on the cross represented the shedding of the blood of the new covenant. People who would regularly repeat this Last Supper would remember the death of Christ for the sacrifice of sins. Jeremiah based his preaching on the prophesied new covenant (Jer. 11:6, 8). Jesus fulfilled the covenant in His death (Matt. 26:28; Mark 14:24; Luke 22:20; 1 Cor. 11:25).

The biblical covenant between God and His people is the basis for covenantal relationships between Christians. The covenant is a demonstration of self-giving, a willingness to seek the best for the other. In the twenty-first century, more pastors will view their call to a church as a covenant. Instead of seeing each church as a rung on the ladder to bigger fields and greener pastures, the church will be a place where the pastor can give of himself as long as God intends for him to stay there.

As a consequence, pastoral tenure will increase in the years ahead. Many pastors will not move unless God's voice is clearly heard to do so. Lifetime pastorates still will not be the norm. Society is so different than 150 years ago that non-lifetime pastorates may still be in the will of God. But ten, twenty, and even thirty-year tenures will become more common.

With more pastors demonstrating a self-giving attitude toward their flocks, tensions between churches and pastors will decline.

Many innocent pastors have been burned because of the sins of predecessors. In time, however, pastoral integrity will be restored and terminations and forced resignations will decline. These factors will also lead to greater mutual respect and, consequently, even longer tenures.

## An Issue of Priorities/A Time of Renewal

The issue is not what is important to pastors. The issue is what is most important to pastors. Leadership seminars, church growth conferences, and books on ministry are still important (I hope so because I lead conferences and seminars and write books!). But the most important agendas on many pastors' calendars in the next several years will be prayer and time in Scripture. And as pastors listen to God more devotedly through prayer and the Bible, the priorities that God has established will become the priorities of ministers.

Pastors encourage their churches to join "together constantly in prayer" (Acts 1:14). They motivate their churches and themselves to be obedient to Great Commission evangelism (Matt. 28:19–20). They will not forsake their families for the ministry of others (1 Tim. 3:5). They will become ambassadors of reconciliation (Matt. 5:23–24). And they will see their flock as Christ sees them: imperfect but perfectly loved.

When the prayer movement began touching lives across our nation, I was unprepared for the affect it would have on pastors. Perhaps the conversation I had with the pastor of a church in Texas will give you some idea of the work God is doing in the pastoral ministry.

The pastor called me because he was struggling in his church. He had attended every possible conference and had purchased a small library of books. "Don't get me wrong," he told me. "I benefited greatly by all those resources. But I knew there had to be something more." The pastor began to pray for God's leadership in discovering "something more." He began to talk with people who had been touched by the prayer movement, and he too began to see prayer as the priority for his ministry.

Soon his priorities began to change and his love for the Savior deepened. Though he still finds time for keeping up with the latest trends in ministry and leadership, he finds his greatest joys in prayer, the Word, his family, and the people in his church. Results and growth are still important; but they are not the most important.

I wish I could report that his church has made a miraculous turnaround, and that it is one the fastest-growing churches in the Southwest. This is not the case. But signs of church renewal are beginning to show themselves. I have no doubt that God will honor this pastor's recommitment in a way that will bring the most glory to the name of Jesus.

The new pastoral model that is emerging is based on Acts 6:1–7. In many senses it is the consequence of the prayer movement and the rediscovery of the Bible. But in other aspects it is a movement unto itself. Watch for significantly changed lives among our spiritual leaders as pastors give greater attention to prayer and the ministry of the Word.

# Chapter 7

# "We Have Found the Messiah . . ."
# Church Trend 7: Evangelistic Renewal
# in the Traditional Church

Evangelism was the very life blood of the early Christians; and so we find that "day by day the Lord added to their number those whom he was saving." It could happen again, if the Church were prepared to pay the price.

—Michael Green

THE CELEBRATION WAS MAGNIFICENT. Excitement abounded. The worship services were intense with celebratory emotions. And accolades poured in from dignitaries in different parts of the country.

Never would pastor Al Capers have believed the amazing success story of Highland Church. When he became pastor ten years earlier, the church was located in an old and declining neighborhood. Average attendance, which had peaked in 1957 at 435, had dipped below 100 for the first time in the church's history.

The church members were very resistant to the idea of ministering to the new people in their neighborhood. Though these words were never heard in public, the sentiment was clear. The neighbors were not "our kind of people." Why, most of these people were not even "our race."

Early in his ministry Pastor Capers started trying to convince the people of Highland Church that a relocation was imperative. Resistance was strong initially. The old building and neighborhood were sentimental favorites, though none of the members had lived in the neighborhood for seven years. Resistance finally broke when attendance consistently stayed under 100. Desperation won over sentimentalism.

It has been several years since the relocation. The move to the east side of town could not have been better timed. New homes began to develop around the church within months after the first building was completed. Pastor Caper's winsome personality and leadership abilities were perfect characteristics to reach the new neighbors. Young families flocked to the church. Growth exploded. Multiple worship services did not solve the space problem. It became inevitable that a new worship center be built. The decision became final when attendance exceeded 450, the highest in the church's history.

And on this beautiful dpring day, the new sanctuary is dedicated with great fanfare. The 800-seat facility is almost filled to capacity. The celebration ends with voices singing together: "To God be the glory, great things he has done . . .."

Al Capers goes home that Sunday afternoon a very delighted man. The success of Highland Church has exceeded all of his expectations. His evangelistic zeal has finally found an outlet through the ministry of this exciting church.

*Evangelism*, Pastor Capers thinks to himself. *Evangelistic emphases have really paid off at this church.* Thinking that he could receive even greater assurances of God's work at Highland, he removes a file from his briefcase that contains the statistical success stories of the church.

Thirty percent increase in attendance in one year. Budget up by nearly 20 percent. Highest attendance in church's history. *Wow, look at this!* He says to himself. *We had 280 new members join in the past twelve months! Unbelievable!*

But one other statistic catches the pastor's eye. Baptisms the past year: 37. The other 243 new members were already Christians. Only 37 people were reached for Christ in one year. He looks further at the resident membership: 814. This meant that one person was reached for Christ annually for every twenty-two members. *That's not effective evangelism*, the pastor ponders. That night Al Capers prayed for wisdom. He could not be satisfied with mere growth; he must seek God's power to foster Kingdom growth.

## Evangelism in The Traditional Church

The great majority of pastors of traditional churches in America would gladly trade places with Al Capers. Sadly, most of these churches are experiencing little or no growth of any kind, much less Kingdom growth.

The story of true evangelistic growth in traditional churches is even sadder. Of the nearly 40,000 Southern Baptist churches in America (most of which could be classified as traditional), 5,596 had *zero* baptisms in 1991, no one reached for Christ![1] And less than 3 percent of the churches baptized fifty or more persons in 1991.[2] Often thought of as one of the most evangelistic denominations, Southern Baptists have much room for improvement.

I need not be too hard on my own denomination. The evangelistic plight of many other church bodies is much worse. Simply stated, churches in America today are as ineffective evangelistically as any point in America's history. And, contrary to conventional wisdom, the evangelistic lethargy is prominent in nontraditional churches as it is in traditional churches. Nontraditional churches with rapid growth tend to have significant transfer growth but low conversion growth. This phenomenon is similar to the experience of growing traditional churches.[3]

The nontraditional church, however, has made a valuable contribution to the cause of evangelism in America. The seeker-church movement, perhaps more than any other recent factor, has caused us to ask ourselves and God if we are doing all that we can to reach the lost for Christ. Let us pause for a moment and reflect on that movement's contributions to evangelism in America.

## Lessons from the Nontraditional Church

My optimism for the evangelistic renewal of traditional churches begins in an unusual place—nontraditional churches. *The most significant contribution of the nontraditional church to the traditional church is the former's insistence that we must win a hearing from the lost and unchurched in our communities.* Many traditional churches have admittedly become ecclesiastical fortresses that require peculiar passwords to enter. The nontraditional church teaches us that we must, at the very least, become aware of "unchurched Harry and Mary," their culture, and how we can reach them.

"Harry and Mary" were invented by Willow Creek Community Church in 1975 as an intentional effort to reach non-Christians in suburban Chicago.[4] In 1993 Lee Strobel, teaching pastor of Willow Creek, wrote a book which shared, in interesting fashion, the Willow Creek philosophy: *Inside the Mind of Unchurched Harry and Mary: How to Reach Friends and Family Who Avoid God and the Church.* Strobel states clearly that he wrote the book "to help advance your understanding of unchurched people so that your personal evangelistic efforts and the efforts of your church might become more effective."[5]

Strobel is well-equipped to write such a book. He considers his former self a prototypical unchurched Harry. He was a promising newspaperman for *The Chicago Tribune* beginning his career in 1974. Strobel writes: "If you were to fast-forward the videotape of my life, zipping past a thirteen-year journalism career, you'd come upon an unlikely picture: a once-cynical and stone-hearted newspaperman preaching the Gospel at a large evangelical church."[6]

The heartbeat of his book is a passion for the lost. Strobel wants to know and share all he can about the unchurched. That passion and vision is making an impact upon the traditional church. This focus, exemplified by Willow Creek and other nontraditional churches, does a great service for the Kingdom. Many traditional churches have become wrapped up in their own programs and traditions to the point that they have forgotten their purpose: evangelizing, ministering, and discipling. It is encouraging to see some traditional churches responding with a renewed desire to discover their communities and the large unchurched population within them.

I do, however, have a deep concern about the manner in which traditional churches are *applying* nontraditional church methods for evangelism. I am not casting stones at a movement that God is using in great ways. Yet I must stress that principle and application are two significantly different matters. The principle of knowing and reaching out to the unchurched is biblical. *How* we do so is a different matter.

Bill Hybels, Lee Strobel, Rick Warren, and other leaders in the seeker-church movement urge pastors and church leaders not to copycat their methodologies. "Understand your own context," they wisely warn eager listeners. While I believe these leaders are sincere in their admonitions, they sometimes contradict their own advice.

For example, in Strobel's book he gives fifteen general observations about the unchurched. I cite six of the fifteen:[7]

- Observation #3: Harry resists rules but responds to reasons.

- Observation #5: Harry has legitimate questions about spiritual matters, but he doesn't expect answers from Christians.

- Observation #7: Harry doesn't just want to know something; he wants to experience it.

- Observation #10: Harry is no longer loyal to denominations, but he is attracted to places where his needs will be met.

- Observation #11: Harry isn't much as a joiner, but he's hungry for a cause he can connect with.

- Observation #15: There's a good chance Harry would try church if a friend invited him—but this may actually do him more harm than good.

The reason I listed these six observations is that I discovered opposite characteristics about the unchurched when I pastored a church in suburban Birmingham. My unchurched Harry responded most readily when we advertised a survey class of the Bible. Birmingham Harry was hungry for knowledge (see observation #7). He *did* expect answers from Christians (observation #5). And he felt "safe" coming to our church because we had "Baptist" in our name (observation #10). Birmingham Harry joined our church within six months (observation #11), and found the traditional church to be a positive experience after he was back in a church routine (observation #15). His personality was one that typically respected rules and authority (observation #3).

The principle of Strobel's book is excellent: know the unchurched and lost so that you can reach them evangelistically. But unchurched Harry/suburban Birmingham is a significantly different person than unchurched Harry/suburban Chicago. The methodologies and approaches to evangelism must be different.

## Further Reasons for Optimism

The influence of the nontraditional church is not the sole reason for optimism. The nontraditional church captured the attention of the traditional church with its focus on the unchurched, but a change of attitude was necessary for traditional church members to have a hunger for evangelism. What has precipitated this new hunger for reaching the lost? Many of the factors we discussed earlier explain the new attitude.

### Prayer and Evangelism

In chapter 1 we examined the remarkable prayer movement that is touching churches of all Christian faiths and approaches to ministry. We also saw that the traditional church has been particularly impacted by this movement. Because the biblical tradition of prayer is being recaptured by these churches, their evangelistic efforts are bearing more fruit daily. Look for a stronger correlation between prayer and evangelism in the twenty-first-century traditional church.

How is prayer specifically related to evangelism? First, traditional church members are praying by name for lost people. One such member tells the amazing story of his church's return to the tradition of true intercessory prayer. The church, located in a small, rural Georgia town, had the typical "who's-who-in-the-hospital" prayer time on Wednesday evening. "We began to dread the service . . . and felt guilty for feeling that way," he said. Attendance was limited to a faithful (guilty?) few.

One deacon decided to research the church's history of Wednesday night prayer meetings. Going through records as much as a century old, he discovered that the mid-week prayer meeting had been one of the most exciting times in the church's life. Its attendance rivaled the Sunday morning crowd. The central element of the prayer meeting was "the prayers for the lost." Specific names and situations of family members, friends, and co-workers were lifted up in intercessory prayer. Not coincidentally, the number of baptisms in the church were at record highs during this time.

The deacon reported this history to the congregation. The church member relating this story claims that he "could almost see faces light up with possibility!" At the conclusion of the report, one faithful member declared that "we must reclaim the great tradition of prayer in our church."

The next Wednesday, a larger-than-usual crowd came to the prayer meeting, some out of conviction, others out of curiosity. For forty-five glorious minutes, nothing but intercessory prayer for the lost took place. Word spread about the exciting prayer time, and the crowds grew steadily.

"Probably the most exciting development took place three months later on a Sunday morning," the church member described with excitement. "We were totally unprepared for what took place. George Carlson, probably one of the meanest sinners in town, came running down the aisle during the invitation to talk with the preacher. You see, George had been one of the people we prayed for every Wednesday, though none of us really expected him to change.

"Well," he continued, "George did not try to keep his voice quiet. Every person in the church heard him say that if he didn't change his ways he thought he'd die on the spot.

"The preacher explained to him the way of Christ and George accepted the Savior right then and there. We all heard him pray out loud: 'I need your forgiveness, Jesus, I accept you. Please come into my life.'

"That's when it happened," the church member explained. "Almost spontaneously the church folks broke out into applause. Then people began standing and clapping and crying and laughing and hugging. Nothing like that *ever* happened in our stuffy church!

"Now we see someone accept Christ almost every week. And, almost always, that person is someone we prayed for. You can't tell me that prayer isn't powerful!"

Not only is directed, intercessory prayer a source of evangelistic power, a true praying church inevitably becomes an evangelistic church. Michael Green, in his classic work on the early church, notes that the praying church became a fellowship of unity and love that attracted the unbelievers: "The fellowship which the Church offered, transcending barriers of race, sex, class, and education, was an enormous attraction."[8]

But even if the fellowship was disrupted, Green notes, quick action was taken lest the evangelistic attraction of the church become diminished: "But the speed and earnestness with which these failures in fellowship were unmasked and reproved by the Christian leaders is eloquent proof of the universal conviction that the extent and power of the Christian outreach depended on the unity and fellowship of the brotherhood. This unity was no dull uniformity."[9]

In *Eating the Elephant*, I featured three traditional churches that had grown against all demographic odds. After studying the churches extensively and interviewing the pastors and church members, I concluded with ten lessons to learn from the churches. First and foremost was lesson one: "Prayer is still the primary church growth principle."[10] C. Peter Wagner agrees. For many years Wagner's books were filled with good methodologies for growth. Now, he says, prayer is the key. "The emergence of exciting possibilities for new and vital prayer ministries in the church is limitless."[11]

Among the three churches I featured in *Eating the Elephant*, Buck Run Baptist Church, located in a rural area outside of Frankfort, Kentucky, had the most dramatic growth. Worship attendance, for example, increased from 120 to 360 from 1990 to 1993, and it has continued to climb since then.

The centerpiece around which everything else revolves at Buck Run is prayer. This traditional church, begun in 1818, is a testimony to the power of prayer. In addition to the regularly-scheduled times of prayer, the church began a Saturday-morning intercessory prayer group called the Eliezer Prayer Fellowship. These intercessors meet at the sanctuary altar and pray specifically for the Sunday worship services. Prayers go forth for the ministers, the musicians, the ushers, and the lost people who will attend. Those lost people are called by name if they are known.

When associate pastor Rob Jackson was asked to evaluate the church's phenomenal growth, he said that it could be explained simply by "the people paying the price in prayer." He further stated that aggressive advertising is not really necessary "when prayers are answered supernaturally. Such a church does not have to beat a lot of drums and sound off blaring sirens to get the attention of the community. The word travels swiftly, and, as Micah 4:1 states, 'The Lord's temple will be established. . . and people will stream to it.'"

## The Bible and Evangelism

The recovery of biblical authority and the new zeal for learning the Bible gives us further reason to expect evangelistic momentum in traditional churches. We noted in chapter two that no great historical, evangelistic awakening has ever taken place without a profound respect for biblical authority and deepened hunger for studying God's Word.

Why does this strong correlation exist between the Bible and evangelism? Why will traditional churches become more fervent about biblical evangelism rather than a quick-fix, shallow, and short-lived methodology?

First, a greater comprehension of the whole counsel of God engenders a profound sense of gratitude for the provision of forgiveness and salvation in Jesus Christ. Michael Green notes that "the enthusiasm to evangelize which marked the early Christians is one of the most remarkable things in the history of religions."[12] These first Christians found "something utterly new, authentic and satisfying."[13] Amazingly, Green notes, "the main motive for evangelism was a theological one."[14] Because these Christians understood theologically what Christ had done for them, their response was evangelism and their motive was gratitude.

In many churches today, no such motive exists because biblical knowledge is so shallow. As we have diluted the gospel and weakened our biblical education opportunities, we have failed to educate our church members about the theological reality of what Christ has done for them. It is little wonder that pleas for evangelistic lifestyles go unheeded.

Listen to Green's assessment of the early church's motive for evangelism: "These men did not spread their message because it was advisable for them to do so, not because it was the socially responsible thing to do. They did not do it primarily for humanitarian or agathistic utilitarian reasons."[15] No, says Green, their motivation was the true understanding of Christology. Theological understanding preceded obedient response: "They did it because of the overwhelming experience of the love of God which they had received through Jesus Christ. The discovery that the ultimate force in the universe was Love, and that this Love had stooped to the very nadir of self-abasement for human good, had an effect on those who believed it which nothing could remove."[16] When biblical truths are comprehended, only the hardest of hearts fail to respond evangelistically. "In a word, Christian evangelism has its motivation rooted in what God is and what he had done for man through the coming and the death and the resurrection of Jesus."[17]

When one grasps both theologically and experientially the sacrifice on the cross, that understanding becomes the greatest single element for evangelistic zeal. But a theological understanding presumes biblical knowledge. The traditional church is recovering the Bible and theology. As a consequence, evangelism will follow naturally and enthusiastically.

Before we move from this subject of evangelism and the Bible, we must note two other motives for evangelism that result from a comprehension of God's Word. If the first motive is gratitude, a close second motive is a sense of responsibility. How could one grasp the essential principles of the New Testament without a resultant desire to "live a life worthy of the Lord and. . . please him in every way: bearing fruit in every good work, growing in the knowledge of God" (Col. 1:10)? As one delves deeper into the riches of Scripture, he or she becomes keenly aware and desirous of obedience—obedience to evangelism in particular. Such was a motive of the early church as well. Green notes that "personal responsibility and accountability before God the sovereign Judge was a prominent spur to evangelism in the early Church."[18]

A final motive for evangelism noted here is a deep concern for lost people. One can not honestly read the pages of Scripture without an unwavering belief that it teaches the exclusivity of salvation through Christ and the reality of an eternal hell for those who reject the Savior.

This deep concern motivated the early church to share the good news of Jesus Christ. Green notes "that concern for the state of the unevangelized was one of the great driving forces behind Christian preaching of the gospel in the early Church."[19] Such a motivation continued for a full century: "This lively awareness of the peril of those without Christ persisted as a major evangelistic motive in the second century. The stress on judgment in the subapostolic writers is so great that it was the subject of ridicule among some pagans."[20] It is interesting to discover that attacking the concept of a literal hell is not a recent development!

On a more contemporary and anecdotal note, I recall vividly the spiritual awakening of a deacon in a church where I served as pastor. The deacon had returned to the study of the Bible with renewed hunger and zeal. Consequently his concern for lost people increased daily. When his next door neighbor was admitted to the hospital with a widespread malignancy, the deacon called me. "Pastor," he nearly shouted, "you have to go to the hospital with me. My neighbor may not make it through the week and I know he is hell-bound!"

The deacon and I shared Christ's way of salvation with the dying man. He received Christ and His forgiveness in a glorious celebration. Less than twelve hours later he died. I was privileged to see first hand how one man's hunger for the Word developed into a concern for lost people. The rediscovery of the Bible by the traditional church will engender a heightened concern for lost people.

## The Unleashed Laity and Evangelism

In the preceding chapter we discussed a movement that is having a profound impact upon thousands of churches: the unleashing of the laity. As the non-ordained in our midst become more and more aware of the God-given privilege and duty to be ministers of the gospel, the army for evangelism will be enlarged by millions.

Interestingly, the Protestant Reformation should have been the beginning of the unleashing of the laity for evangelism. The reformers themselves saw this possibility. Some believe the reformers did not have an interest in evangelism because of their strong doctrines of election and predestination. "On the contrary," notes

Reformation theologian Timothy George, "all of the reformers were concerned with confronting individuals with the claims of Christ and with calling them to repent and believe the gospel."[21]

Unfortunately, this full-church impetus for evangelism was thwarted by an anti-missionary view which limited the missionary mandate to the original apostles only. Johann Gerhard, a seventeenth-century proponent of this view, believed the world had already heard the gospel during the apostolic age. There was no need to offer it to them again. "This idea trickled down to the level of popular piety and was reflected in an anti-missionary hymn which made the rounds in the eighteenth century:

> Go into all the world,
> the Lord of old did say,
> But now where He has planted thee,
> there thou shouldst stay.[22]

Fortunately, the anti-missionary forces were replaced by a new zeal for carrying the gospel to the corners of the world. Denominations and missionary societies centered their activity around the work of home and foreign missionaries.

While we applaud this evangelistic emphasis, we must look with concern at a corollary issue. With the focus on missionaries and pastors in the pulpit, a mindset formed that said specialists would do the work of evangelism. The laity should give to mission funds and pay the preacher, but only those "called persons" would carry out the proclamation of the gospel and witness to the lost.

It was the traditional church in the 1960s that began to counter the "clergy-only" evangelism mindset. First traditional church members began utilizing the tools of parachurch organizations to train non-ordained men and women to share their faith. Then some churches developed their own evangelism training tools. *Evangelism Explosion*, devised by D. James Kennedy at Coral Ridge Presbyterian Church in Ft. Lauderdale, Florida, won wide acceptance in many evangelical churches. Other training programs soon followed.

While these tools were very useful in unleashing the laity for evangelism, their effectiveness was limited. Rarely did more than 5 to 10 percent of church members participate in witness training.[23] Some of the laity became involved, but the great majority remained on the sidelines.

But a new day is dawning. More and more laity in traditional churches are doing ministry. As the traditional church leads in unleashing the laity to do ministry, there will be an evangelistic renewal. Instead of motives of guilt and program participation, the motives will be more in line with those of the early church: gratitude, a sense of biblical responsibility, and a deep concern for lost people.

## Institutional Decline

The reasons for optimism about evangelistic renewal stated thus far are noble in nature: prayer, hunger for the Bible, and the unleashing of the laity. One final reason must be mentioned that is less noble in motive. Many traditional churches have experienced membership and budget declines for years. In an effort to save these churches, some leaders have seen evangelism as their last hope for institutional survival. Two outcomes generally take place.

In some instances the institutional decline is a wake-up call for the church. The members begin to wonder if "the way they have always done it" is the best way. They recognize their weakened commitment to prayer and the Bible, and their idolatrous commitment to ineffective programs and methods. A sense of corporate repentance envelopes the fellowship. The church dreams again about God's work in their midst. Consequently, outreach and evangelism take on a renewed life and commitment. The church is renewed.

In other cases the decline precipitates a call for a new program or methodology. The hottest church growth tool is implemented with high hopes and dubious commitment. The new program is viewed as salvific. At best, however, a blip of growth is short-lived. Continued decline is inevitable.

I am amazed at the number of books and articles written about declining churches. In many of these writings, methodologies and new programs are panacea. Nothing more than lip service is given to spiritual truths and the need for prayer and a commitment to the total truthfulness and obedience of God's Word. We should welcome books highlighting the best of contemporary methodologies, but such tools most never stand alone. They must be built upon the foundation of Spirit-led and Christ-centered truths.

## The Traditional Church Model of Evangelism

In a few pages I will share with you a new model of evangelism that is emerging in many traditional churches. Before we see this development, let us briefly review the models of evangelism most common in both traditional and nontraditional churches. The traditional model of church evangelism can be expressed in various forms, but it typically has five key elements.

## Development of Relationships

Although some advocates of nontraditional churches imply that their churches are the only ones that focus on relationship evangelism, traditional churches have been doing so for years. No matter what type of church I have surveyed over the past several years, at least three-fourths of the new converts (one year or less) said that their relationship to the church and ultimately to Christ began with the friendship of a Christian.

## Outreach Programs

Evangelism in traditional churches is typically organized programmatically. "Monday night outreach" or "Tuesday visitation" is still a common expression. With the exception of a small minority of churches, participation in these programs is sparse.

## Evangelism Training Programs

A recent development of the past thirty years has been the explosion of evangelism training programs. We already mentioned *Evangelism Explosion* developed by D. James Kennedy. A later addition for Southern Baptists was *Continuous Witness Training*. Many churches have trained their members in tract evangelism, using material from parachurch organizations like Campus Crusade for Christ.

A common criticism of these programs is that they are "canned" — impersonal and rigid. While this may be true, critics fail to realize that many Christians have no idea how to share their faith with others. The freedom and excitement for Christ expressed by participants in these programs is immeasurable. And critics notwithstanding, thousands of people have met the Savior through these presentations.

## Confrontational Evangelism

These two words often carry negative connotations. To confront, in the minds of many, means to be heavy-handed and threatening. In its true biblical sense, however, confrontation is positive and mandated. Jesus' confrontation of the woman at the well (John 4:1–26) was done in love and concern. The woman was confronted with her lostness and the way of salvation. Traditional churches typically advocate that the communication of the good news is not complete until people hear that they are lost and are told that Christ is their only hope and salvation.

### Cold-Call Evangelism

Another expression of traditional church evangelism is cold-call evangelism. "Cold" means that no prior relationship with the lost person has been established. He or she is presented a "plan of salvation" as a total stranger.

Although this method of evangelism has come under increasing fire, it is not very difficult to build a biblical defense for witnessing to strangers. Again the woman at the well is a good example of evangelism without a prior relationship established. And the apostolic patterns of evangelism often included meetings between strangers (for example, Philip and the Ethiopian eunuch, Acts 8:26–39).

The critics are right to urge sensitivity when evangelizing strangers. Today it is increasingly difficult to get an audience with someone we do not know. It is still imperative, however, that Christians be prepared to share their faith with a stranger, because the opportunity to establish a relationship will not always avail itself.

## The Nontraditional Church Model of Evangelism

The nontraditional church offers some different perspectives on evangelism. As is the case for traditional churches, all churches in one category are not monolithic. Still, the nontraditional church typically expresses its evangelism in five common themes.

### Development of Relationships

Like the traditional church, the nontraditional church urges believers in the fellowship to develop relationships with unbelievers. The underlying premise is that an unbeliever will develop a relationship with a believer long before he or she will establish a relationship with the church.

One key in this process is to eventually invite the unbeliever to a worship service. This is where he or she will begin to hear the gospel message.

## Worship as the Front Door

A fascinating development in the nontraditional church is the strategy to evangelize and bring people into the church first through the worship services. This evangelistic strategy has been called "worship as the front door."[24] The greatest allocation of resources go into planning, rehearsing, and preparing for one or more major worship services each week. Whereas the traditional church reaches out into the community by visiting in homes and taking surveys door-to-door, the nontraditional church focuses its attention on the worship services. Of course, these churches have the expectation that their members will invite the unchurched to worship on a regular basis.

## Seeker-friendly Services

"Seeker" is the nomenclature given to an unbeliever who visits a church worship service. Everything that takes place during these services keeps in mind that unbelievers are present. Because they may not understand traditional liturgies, hymns, or sermons, an intentional effort is made to be "seeker-friendly" or "seeker-sensitive." Hymnals may not be used. Sermons may be couched in easy-to-understand, practical-living principles. Anonymity is always provided. Every possible effort is made not only to hold the seeker's attention, but also to avoid offending him or her at all costs.

Quality becomes job one in seeker-friendly services. These church leaders are aware that seekers are of the television generation. They are used to fast-moving, slick, and exciting productions. The worship service must match the appeal of the movies and television shows seekers watch. Everything in the service moves quickly. Only the best musicians sing and play. The best actors and actresses provide dramatic stories. And every technical aspect, from the sound system to the lighting system, is planned with precision and quality. The worship service must keep the attention of those unbelievers who visit the church.

## Event Evangelism

Nontraditional churches will also use big events to draw unbelievers into their churches. The event may use a big-name speaker or musician, or it may be related to a known need, i.e. a seminar entitled "Recovering the Joy in Marriages." The principles are similar to those in seeker-friendly worship services. An attempt is made to use the events as an evangelistic front door.

## Deliberate Attempts Not to Confront

This evangelistic strategy is where traditional and nontraditional churches demonstrate the most significant difference. A traditional church is deliberately confrontive. In its presentation of the gospel, from evangelistic teams to a public invitation, traditional church evangelistic strategy seeks a decision. To the contrary, the nontraditional church deliberately avoids "forcing" a decision. The atmosphere of the nontraditional church is one of comfort for the seeker. Confrontation may cause the unbeliever to leave, never to return. The premise behind the seeker-sensitive church is to allow the lost person time and space until he or she is ready to make a decision without coercion.

## The Traditional Church Model of Evangelism in the Twenty-first Century

Perhaps the most amazing aspect of evangelistic strategy for the traditional church in the twenty-first century is how similar it will look to the late twentieth-century model. Traditional outreach or visitation will make a comeback in its acceptance. For many churches this will mean a certain day or evening when the congregation "gathers to go."

Now this traditional outreach will be revised a bit. For example, the telephone will be used more than the automobile. Unexpected visits may be altogether replaced by invitations to dinner. Still the church will have a sense of "going," of corporate obedience to the Great Commission.

Because traditional church leaders have heard repeatedly that "visitation" is ineffective, many have abandoned or de-emphasized their outreach ministries. This is an unfortunate development, because every statistical study of traditional outreach and evangelistic growth has shown a strong correlation between the two.[25] The dogmatic statements of the ineffectiveness of traditional outreach are simply not supported by the facts.

Secondly, traditional churches will continue to emphasize confrontational evangelism. Now we know that obnoxious, collar-grabbing, blue-face-screaming "Are you saved, brother?" is not only ineffective but socially offensive. Fortunately, that stereotype of confrontational evangelism is rare.

It would appear that the traditional church's confrontational approach has weightier biblical support than the nonconfrontational approach of the nontraditional church. The gospel is confrontive by its very nature. And the Savior was confrontive as He declared without hesitation that "unless he is born again, he cannot see the kingdom of God" (John 3:3).

The major shift in traditional church outreach and evangelism will not be in methodologies, but in the emphasis on spiritual factors. When a methodology appears dead, two alternatives are available. The first is to have a funeral and never be bothered with the corpse again. The second is to have a resurrection, and give new life and purpose to an old and lifeless methodology.

The problem with many of the traditional church methodologies may not be the methodologies per se. It may be that, in slow and subtle progression, the methodology became an end instead of a means. In the process, prayer and dependence on God for successes were sacrificed to a god of the ages—"the-way-we've-always-done-it" god.

Now some critics will say we cannot do traditional outreach because our world has changed so very much. But the world does not dictate the church's behavior. As Paul urged the church at Rome, "Do not conform any longer to the pattern of this world" (Rom. 12:2).

The next century will bring to traditional churches a new harvest of souls and a new zeal for evangelism. The church will not forsake the obedient response of going (Matt. 28:19). And it will go in power as God's people are unleashed to do ministry—delving daily in the riches of Scripture and building all evangelism and outreach upon the immeasurable power of prayer.

# Chapter 8

# "Therefore Go . . ."
# Church Trend 8:
# The Explosion of Church Planting

The early church knew little of isolated converts drifting from a local church fellowship. This brings me to believe that the express purpose of evangelists and apostles during the apostolic age was to see local churches planted in ever increasing numbers all over the known world. They were not occupied, as are so many today, with doing evangelism that took no practical thought of what would become of converts.

—Samuel D. Faircloth

CHURCH PLANTING IS ONE of the most exciting ministries in which we can be involved. Church planting is one of the most dangerous ministries in which we can be involved. I know both facts from experience.

The church I formerly pastored, Green Valley Baptist Church, is located in a rather affluent suburb of Birmingham, Alabama. In the second year of my ministry at the church, I began to notice a pattern in our growth. We were reaching young adults whose households would be demographically classified as middle class and upper middle class. (I hesitated to call them "yuppies" because their spiritual values were significantly higher than the stereotypical yuppie.)

I believe that the people of Green Valley were sincerely open to reaching all kinds of people. I never once detected a mindset that said we should only seek "our kind of people." But, despite the best efforts and attitudes, we continued to reach the same type of people. Even when a person of a different socioeconomic background visited our church, he or she rarely returned. We were living proof of the homogenous unit principle despite our sincere efforts to break out of our homogeneity.

My staff and I began to hear God's voice about possible means to reach other people. Eventually we sensed God's affirmation of our desire to start a satellite church in another location about three miles from the main church facility. We would reach others and also develop a more contemporary worship service from our existing church.

After several months of prayer, planning, presentations, and proposals, Green Valley South was born. Those days of preparation were among the most exciting of my ministry. A sense of apostolic heritage and a cutting-edge future made all of us feel as if we were part of something great for God.

But I must also admit that those days were among the most frustrating and draining of my ministry. Opposition to the concept started from within the church. I was ill-prepared for the intensity by which some members opposed this initiative.

The greatest surprise came when other churches in the community expressed their opposition to the proposed church. My naivete about churches working together for the Kingdom was quickly shattered. I still have a lengthy letter from a pastor who protested to me and every deacon in our church. His letter was filled with concern for his own church in an area that was 60 to 70 percent unchurched. Although Green Valley South has since experienced steady growth, it has not drawn one member from the concerned pastor's church.

As the dean of a school whose focus is Great Commission ministries, I tell our students interested in church planting to prepare for the most exciting *and* the most challenging days of their lives. Interestingly, in our school the level of interest in church planting is soaring. This is a nationwide trend  that could change the landscape of American Christianity.

A part of this growing interest in church planting comes from leaders in traditional churches who never considered starting another church. If this momentum continues, i.e. traditional churches starting new churches, the twenty-first century will be the greatest century of church planting ever.

## Do We Really Need More Churches?

"I drive four miles to attend this church," the member protested. "And I must pass at least ten or more churches to get here. I know for a fact that many of those churches are really struggling. The last thing we need is another church. We need to build up these other churches first — including our own!"

That voice of protest was registered at the business meeting where we proposed to start a new church. It is perhaps the most common objection raised by Christians who are concerned about new churches. Are such objections valid? Do we really need new churches? Can we be better stewards of people, time, and money by stimulating growth in existing churches rather than starting new ones?

In 1820, our nation's population was 9.6 million. With nearly 11,000 congregations the new nation had one church for 875 residents.[1] By 1860, an aggressive four decades of church planting resulted in a fivefold increase in churches to 54,000. With the population now 31.6 million, a church was available for every 600 residents.

Unfortunately the trend toward more churches per capita stopped in 1860. By 1990 the ratio of churches to the population remained about the same, despite the passage of 130 years.

## The Growing Unchurched Population

A more important consideration than the ratios of churches to the population is the number of Americans who do not attend church at all. In the last quarter of a century our nation has become a true mission field as a growing percentage of the population dropped out of church involvement. One of the consequences of this trajectory is that as many as 85 percent of all churches in America are either plateaued or declining.[2] In 1988, church growth expert Win Arn declared that 71 percent of the total U.S. population is either unaffiliated with any religion or are Christians in "name only."[3] George Gallup's study in the same year showed that 44 percent of the population is solidly unchurched.[4]

C. Peter Wagner estimates that the unchurched population in America may be as high as 55 percent. Citing Wagner in an interview, *Christianity Today* notes, "He points to the fact that in spite of church growth's advances in the eighties, the percentage of American adults attending church has remained almost the same (about 45 percent), while Protestant church membership has actually declined."[5]

## Who Are the Unchurched?

The baby boomer generation accounts for the greatest number of unchurched Americans. The reasons for this phenomenon are twofold and straightforward. First, the boomers are the largest generation in America's history. Those persons born between 1946 and 1964 number over 76 million and represent one-third of the total population. Second, the boomers were the first American generation to abandon the church in such extraordinary numbers. Enough has been written about this over-studied generation to fill a library. The boomers say that the church is irrelevant to them, so the average boomer attends church only six times a year.[6] Of course, included in that number are boomers who do not attend church at all and some who are very faithful attenders.

While we were correct in listening to the boomers' plea for relevancy, somewhere in the process the church went overboard. As churches experimented with models to attract this generation, we succeeded in bringing many back into the fold. But, ironically, that which attracted them did not hold them. The great boomer return eventually became the great boomer exodus.

After returning to the church, many boomers became disillusioned and bored. What was once exciting and even entertaining became superficial and common. The boomers went to the churches seeking something different that would make a difference in their lives. What they found were many churches that were hardly different from the unchurched world from which they came.

The newly-planted churches of the next century still have an opportunity to reach this aging generation. But the great movements of prayer and biblical depth must be a part of their evanglism. Relevancy again will be a key. More importantly, however, will be biblical substance and people who have not bowed to gods of this age.

The baby busters and their children represent another significant portion of the unchurched population. What is perhaps most significant about the busters is that they are a second generation of unchurched people. For many of the busters and their children, the experience of church is unknown. An article in the *Dallas Morning News* speaks of this religious gap when telling the story of boomer parents who decided to return to church. Their pilgrimage was a return based upon their young son's confusion.

Blake, four years old at the time, had spent the night with his grandparents. The next morning the grandparents were preparing for worship services when the parents came to get their son. Blake, however, insisted on staying longer, saying his grandparents were "going to Church's and I want to stay for fried chicken."[7] The child's concept of "church" was a fried chicken fast food chain!

Many traditional churches in the years ahead will see such generations as true pagan mission fields. They will consequently have a zeal to reach the unchurched with the same enthusiasm as churches had for foreign missions in the nineteenth and early twentieth centuries. This zeal will manifest itself in thousands of new churches.

## The Southern Baptist Example

C. Peter Wagner believes that the Southern Baptist Convention's rise to be the largest Protestant denomination is directly tied to church planting. Wagner comments, "One of their secrets is that they constantly invest substantial resources of personnel and finances in church planting on all levels from local congregations to associations to state conventions to their Home Mission Board in Atlanta."[8]

My denomination is a good example of the critical importance of church planting for the next century. We could offer plenty of excuses for lack of growth. For example, our denomination seems to be involved in some type of controversy or debate on an ongoing basis. Regardless of one's position, these controversies distract from missions and evangelism.

On another note, one could see the Southern Baptists as a maturing denomination sheerly because of its size and age. Inertia in such a massive body could be expected. Or perhaps one could point to the number of churches that have disbanded, merged, or withdrawn from the convention. Between four and five churches *per week* are dropped from Southern Baptist records.

Any one of these reasons might be sufficient to suspect that the denomination is declining. But, to the contrary, the Southern Baptist Convention continues to grow. The rate of growth has admittedly slowed, but nevertheless, growth continues.

This growth from a statistical viewpoint can be explained by one factor: church planting. About ten new Southern Baptist churches are started each week. Consequently the denomination gains approximately five new churches net per week (see Table 8.1 on the following page).

Even more remarkable than the number of constituted churches is the number of newly-started congregations (Not all congregational starts become constituted churches). Southern Baptists have

### Table 8.1: Annual Change in the
### Number of Southern Baptist Churches

Source: Strategic Information and Planning Section, The Baptist Sunday School Board. SBC, Nashville, TN.

| Year | First Time Reporting | Reorganized | Dropped | Net Change |
|------|------|------|------|------|
| 1973 | 323 | 19 | 211 | 131 |
| 1974 | 338 | 20 | 289 | 69 |
| 1975 | 395 | 28 | 255 | 168 |
| 1976 | 372 | 22 | 223 | 171 |
| 1977 | 373 | 42 | 233 | 182 |
| 1978 | 28 | 28 | 231 | 149 |
| 1979 | 395 | 27 | 221 | 201 |
| 1980 | 403 | 25 | 202 | 226 |
| 1981 | 431 | 22 | 205 | 248 |
| 1982 | 436 | 21 | 234 | 223 |
| 1983 | 413 | 17 | 201 | 229 |
| 1984 | 450 | 13 | 254 | 209 |
| 1985 | 458 | 17 | 236 | 239 |
| 1986 | 433 | 10 | 306 | 137 |
| 1987 | 404 | 14 | 248 | 170 |
| 1988 | 472 | 7 | 198 | 281 |
| 1989 | 434 | 9 | 225 | 218 |
| 1990 | 445 | 13 | 269 | 189 |
| 1991 | 454 | 24 | 231 | 247 |
| 1992 | 497 | 17 | 248 | 266 |
| 1993 | 499 | 8 | 250 | 257 |

started *3.3 new congregations per day for the past ten years*. And under the leadership of Charles Chaney, vice-president of the Southern Baptist Home Mission Board, the denomination has set a goal to start four new congregations per day for the 1990s.[9]

If the denomination reaches its goal, Southern Baptists will have 50,000 congregations by A.D. 2000. By 1990 the convention had surpassed 43,600 in total churches and church-type missions.[10] Chaney estimates that by the end of the century, Southern Baptists will have 14,000 ethnic and predominately black congregations.[11]

One of the reasons many traditional churches decline and die is that they fail to reproduce themselves. It was never the New Testament pattern for a church to keep to itself.

The first church where believers were called Christians was at Antioch (Acts 11:26). The church experienced remarkable growth as many people accepted Christ (Acts 11:24). But the church at Antioch never saw itself as a fellowship content to keep the people in one location. They were a *sending* church; they sent Barnabas and Saul off on the mission of starting and encouraging new churches (Acts 13:1–3).

That consideration, more than any single factor, explains why we need new churches. The biblical pattern of churches is that they reproduce themselves continually. The local church is mandated by God's Word to reproduce itself again and again. A church that ceases to multiply is no longer a healthy church. One of the key reasons that churches become extinct is that they have no children or grandchildren.

## Seven Reasons Traditional Churches Will Experience an Explosion of Church Planting

The twenty-first century will be a new era of church planting, with long-established churches leading the way. At least seven signs point to this phenomenon.

### 1. The Great Prayer Movement

I recently attended Little Flock Baptist Church, a rapidly growing church south of Louisville, Kentucky. During the service the pastor, Ronald Shaver, asked for a time of prayer for harvesters. He reminded the people that Christians often spend their evangelistic prayer time praying for lost persons. But, he said, Jesus told them to pray for workers for the harvest. The lost people, he explained, were waiting for workers to come to them: "Then he said to his disciples, 'The harvest is plentiful but the workers are few. Ask the Lord of the harvest, therefore, to send out workers into his harvest field'" (Matt. 9:37–38).

Little Flock Baptist Church is but another church that is being touched by the prayer movement. God specifically led this church to pray for workers for the harvest. Praying churches across America are following this exciting trend.

One development of this praying trend will be new churches. As God honors the prayer for workers, He will do so by sending many out into the fields. In the gospel of Matthew the sending out of the twelve disciples follows the prayer for workers (Matt. 10:1–42). Never are workers for the harvest told to stay in their local congregations. They are always sent out. Prayer will bring forth "apostles" to start churches. I believe the gift of the apostle is the gift of being sent out. The Greek word for apostle literally means "one sent out." One of the significant fruits of the prayer movement will be more workers sent out for the harvest by starting new churches.

### 2. The Laity Unleashed

In the fifth chapter we examined the exciting trend of the "new reformation," the unleashing of the laity for ministry. When our church planted Green Valley South, an amazing amount of lay-ministry energy was unleashed. Some of the members of our main campus had never been able to utilize fully their gifts and talents until they were able to be part of a church planting team. I was fascinated to watch these people perform an unbelievable level of ministry.

Before one of my associate pastors began to function as pastor of the new church, the newly-planted mission was virtually leaderless. Although I preached at the new campus, my duties as senior pastor of the other church limited the time I gave to Green Valley South. Amazingly, the church did quite well without my guidance. The laypeople really took charge of the ministry. (It was also humbling to know that the church could survive without me!)

As great numbers of believers are unleashed to do the work of ministry, many will be drawn to church planting. In fact, some laypersons will have a lifetime of voluntary ministry starting new churches. And since new churches have a higher evangelistic growth rate than older churches, more people will be won to Christ.[12]

### 3. Longer-term Pastorates

An almost unspoken reason exists that explains why many pastors do not lead their churches to start new churches. Church planting requires giving up money and members, at least in the short run.

146

For pastors who must have a numerically successful track record in one single location for their own career advancement, church planting is never considered a viable option. Furthermore, because the starting of new churches requires so much energy, these pastors would rather devote their personal and church's resources to build up their own local congregation.

With the shift in pastoral paradigm to an Acts 6 model, this concern will no longer be an issue for many pastors. Upward mobility, in a secular sense, will not be a driving force. Instead of concerning themselves with career advancement, the new paradigm pastor will be more concerned about Great Commission obedience.

This new biblical focus means that pastors will have a Kingdom perspective more than a local church perspective. They will not "lose" members in a Kingdom sense. The churches will instead send members so that more can be added to the Kingdom.

Is such a trend likely? After all, for decades many pastors have measured their own worthiness by the size of their congregations. Can we really expect a new era of pastors whose passion is obedience instead of promotion? Two major indicators tell us that such a hope is realistic.

The first is anecdotal but convincing evidence that prayer is returning as a pastoral priority. I am a member of Springdale Church, a Southern Baptist church in Louisville, Kentucky. Pastor David Butler's sermon the Sunday before I wrote this chapter was "Ten Reasons Why Christians Should Have a Quiet Time with God." His entire message was excellent, but one particular point made me listen even more attentively. Pastor Butler shared a confessional testimony: "Before I entered the ministry, I would have dynamic quiet times with God. Sometimes those quiet times could be measured in hours instead of minutes." He paused for a moment, then continued: "But when I entered the ministry, I became too busy for those quiet times. Isn't that something? Because of the ministry, I became too busy for God! We who are in full-time vocation ministry must return to a priority of prayer."

David Butler's words are being repeated in pulpits across America. These ministers are not critical of methodologies. They are simply concerned that busywork has replaced the priority of prayer. And many of these pastors are becoming models for prayer themselves.

An inevitable promise of prayer is obedience, including an obedience to start churches. Reproducing churches will thus become a consequence of praying churches.

A second indicator of the new paradigm pastor's desire to start new churches is found in the seminary and Bible college classrooms across America. The number one vocational interest of the students in the school where I serve as dean is church planting. A new generation of pastors will soon be leading churches, in unprecedented fashion, to start new churches.

### 4. A Renewed Missionary Zeal

A number of amazing similarities can be noted between the first century A.D. culture and the culture in America today. Two words characterize both cultures: pagan and pluralistic. Christians are in the minority; and the Christian faith competes with a variety of other belief systems. In America twenty-five years ago the question to Christians was: Does your God exist? Today the question is: How is your God different from the other gods? The uniqueness or exclusiveness of the Christian faith is seriously doubted by many Americans.

The early church faced that same obstacle. The apostle Paul himself addressed the issue of pluralism when he gave his sermon about the "unknown god" in Athens at the Areopagus (Acts 17:16–34). Indeed the believers in the early church responded to the realities of paganism and pluralism by sending missionaries like Paul and Barnabas to different areas. And as they preached the gospel message, people were won to Christ and churches were started.

Many churches in America today are waking up to the fact that lost people will not flood the doors of their facilities. Any hope whatsoever to reach many of them will be with new churches that can identify with those on the outside. And many churches are catching that missionary zeal. They are no longer content to send missions offerings only. They are giving more financially to missions and starting new churches. They are discovering that their God is not a God of limited resources. When they give of the resources of money, people, or time, God honors their gifts and supplies abundantly.

## 5. The Desire to Reach New Cultures

Home Mission Board vice-president Charles Chaney notes that the Southern Baptist Convention will have 10,000 ethnic congregations and 4,000 congregations in predominantly black communities by the year 2000.[13] This is an amazing development for a denomination whose origins include issues of race. In fact, Southern Baptists probably would not be growing numerically if it were not for the non-white congregations.

The American church is waking up to the fact that their fellowship cannot reach the wide variety of cultural and ethnic groups in our nation. Some of the churches and denominations are, admittedly, responding only to precipitous and long-term declines. But even the motive of survival can be used to reach people groups for Christ.

One particularly exciting trend in this type of church planting is a positive response to changing communities. For many years the response of churches located in neighborhoods that have changed from all white to mostly non-white has been to die a slow death or to close down and move to an all-white suburb. The net result has been the loss of a Christian witness in the community.

Today many churches are responding positively in two different ways. A small number of congregations are giving the leadership responsibilities of the church to the new residents. I consulted with a church in Florida whose attendance had dropped dramatically when African-Americans moved into the neighborhood and whites exited in large numbers. Though most of the whites had left the area surrounding the church, slightly over 100 decided that they would not let their church die. When a pastoral vacancy occurred, the all-white church called an African-American pastor. Eventually the black community began to sense that the church was "theirs." Within two years the church was growing again, but this time with a majority of the church being African-American. In essence a new church was planted in anticipation of the death of another church.

A more common occurrence today is the sale or gift of a church in a transition neighborhood. In Birmingham, Alabama, Hunter Street Baptist Church's attendance had declined to the point where most everyone in the church realized that death was imminent. But nearby Sardis Baptist Church was bursting at the seams as the African-American church reached the community—now mostly black. Had nothing taken place, Hunter Street would have closed, and Sardis would have been limited because of its small facilities.

But in an arrangement beneficial to both groups, Hunter Street sold its facilities to Sardis. Hunter Street then moved to the Birmingham suburb of Hoover. And in 1994, less than ten years later, Sardis has an average attendance approaching one thousand while Hunter Street now exceeds two thousand in attendance. In essence two new churches were planted though both existed prior to their relocation. Hunter Street Baptist Church particularly was a church plant because it was just a few short years from death.

### 6. Alternative Worship Styles

Shortly after his departure from Keith Community Church, pastor Phillip Lewis shared with me his frustrations that ultimately led to his resignation. A significant number of the younger adults had complained about the "slow and boring" worship services. They wanted to invite their friends, but they were afraid their friends would feel the same about the worship services.

As the church leadership began discussing a more contemporary worship service, the fights began. Never had such heated emotions emerged in the church's history.

In the next chapter we will look more extensively at a major trend that is emerging in worship service styles. For now we will simply acknowledge that changes in the worship service often generate enormous conflict. James Emery White says, "Growing churches which have transitioned their church to non-traditional forms of music have often, as a result, received enormous criticism."[14] Elmer Towns agrees that worship styles are the source of greatest controversy in churches today.[15] And Russell Chandler sees the debate continuing: "Nowhere is the dissonance greater than in discussions about what's 'proper' in 'Christian' music."[16]

Phillip Lewis decided to try to please everyone. He proposed moving the traditional service to 8:30 A.M. The 10:45 A.M. service would be a contemporary worship service. The later time would benefit the young adults who had to get children ready on Sunday mornings. With some acrimony still remaining, Keith Community Church made the transition to two worship services.

For two months there was peace in the church family. The younger adults were particularly happy with the new contemporary format. They invited their friends and growth was obvious. Then the murmuring began again.

Those in the early service missed the later worship time they had enjoyed for years. "Why were we the ones who had to move?" they began to murmur. Furthermore, the multiple worship services left many vacant pews. And their service was not experiencing growth.

The murmur turned into a roar as the traditionalists threatened to withdraw their financial support. Phillip Lewis decided that the fight was not worth it, so the single worship service returned. But this time no one was happy with him, so his resignation became inevitable.

Another trend that is accentuating the growth of church planting is the realization that America's great cultural diversity often manifests itself in worship-style preferences. Sometimes it is simply not possible to please everyone in a single location, so a new church is started.

When I was pastor in Birmingham, one of the reasons we started a satellite church was to offer a church with a contemporary worship style. One location had hymnals; the other did not. One location had a choir; the other had a praise team. One location had an organ and piano; the other had a variety of instruments. One location had padded pews; the other had padded folding chairs.

American missionaries to foreign mission fields have long recognized the need to contextualize, or to adapt culturally to their mission field. American churchgoers must realize that our nation is culturally diverse, and new churches are needed to offer worship services in the culture that is being reached.

Several of my students at Southern Seminary are serving churches with a variety of worship styles: liturgical, traditional, blended, and contemporary. One of them actually started a church in Indiana where the service and the music is designed for country and country-gospel music lovers! The increase in new churches in the twenty-first century will be, in part, a response to our national cultural diversity.

## 7. Refocused Denominational Leadership

In the early pages of this book, I mentioned that we would see a neo-denominational era in the twenty-first century. Those denominations that will prosper will view their role as servants and resources for the local church. The denominations will exist for the churches, a "bottom-up" view that has not been prevalent in many bodies.

One major role of successful denominations will be leadership in church planting. I already referred to Charles Chaney of the Home Mission Board of the Southern Baptist Convention, and his key role in leading Southern Baptist churches to start new churches. Larry Lewis is president of the Home Mission Board and he, too, is providing key leadership for Southern Baptist church planting. But, says Lewis, church planting is not done for the benefit of the denomination: "However, the reason we start new churches throughout America and around the world is not to reach a denominational goal or to fulfill some denominational program."[17] The goal is obedience says Lewis: "Our purpose is to fulfill the Great Commission by establishing Bible-preaching soul-winning, ministering churches everywhere there are people."[18]

But Lewis realizes that the leadership to start new churches best belongs in the hands of local churches and their pastors. He adds, "Every pastor must seek a vision from the Lord as to where new congregations need to be established in his area."[19]

In the years ahead we will see more denominational leaders with hearts for fulfilling the Great Commission through church planting. The denomination can enhance the process by encouragement, equipping, and provision of resources. Their role is, and will be even more so in the future, a partnership with local churches.

## Seven Ways Traditional Churches Will Plant New Churches

The traditional church of the twenty-first century will establish new churches in a variety of ways. Though it may sound like an oxymoron, "innovative traditional" churches will be at the forefront. Let us examine seven ways these new churches will be established.

### 1. Traditional

The traditional model of church planting will still be a healthy model in the twenty-first century. With this model, a sponsoring church or churches send a nucleus of members to start a new church in another geographical area. The new church is usually located within driving distance of the sponsoring church. The goal is for the new church to become totally autonomous as soon as possible. The success rate of these new churches is relatively high. Members of the nucleus are typically dedicated givers and workers. Because of the strong financial and member base, the chances of survival are good.

The disadvantage of the traditional approach is the reluctance or perceived inability of the sponsoring church to "give up" members and money. Many churches exist for a century or more without ever starting a new work.

## 2. Colonization

Colonization is identical to the traditional model with one major exception. The nucleus of members sent by the parent church relocate to a distant geographical area. Those members must sell their homes, find new jobs, and send their children to new schools. A radical level of commitment to the Great Commission is a requisite. For these and other practical reasons, colonization is a rare form of church planting.

## 3. Adoption

A successful church in Texas heard of three area churches that had made a decision to close their doors. The pastor of the thriving church made a commitment to provide the people, the funds, and the leadership to keep the churches open. Though new churches were not planted, three churches were kept alive and the impact was similar. While it is easier to have babies than to raise the dead, God uses mission-minded leaders to resurrect dying churches.

## 4. Satellite

For many the satellite model is the most exciting development in church planting. John Vaughn describes this method in his book, The Large Church: "Large churches with satellite groups combine the best of two growth strategies. . . . Although many of these churches are committed to building a large central church, most are just as committed to penetrating and reaching the city through the use of small groups coordinated fully, in most instances, by the parent congregation."[20]

The satellite model is similar to the secular model of branch banking. Each new location has a high degree of autonomy, but it is still part of the same church. In other words, there is one church with many locations. This method may be the major method of church planting in America in the twenty-first century. The new church location can reach a new geographic area but still have all the combined resources of the parent and other satellite churches. This model also engenders accountability. Each of the locations looks to one another to start new churches. This mutual account-ability to the vision of church planting is probably the single greatest strength of the satellite model.

## 5. Multicongregational

The multicongregational model of church planting allows the start of a new church in the facility of an existing church. This method works well in a multi-ethnic area. An English-speaking church, for example, could share its facilities with Korean and Chinese churches. Each church uses the building at different hours. The different groups may choose to be autonomous, or they may decide to be subgroups of a larger, single church. This model is one of good stewardship, since several churches can exist in just one facility.

A variation of the multicongregational model takes place when a church decides to develop intentionally new congregations within its own fellowship. Josh Hunt has been a significant proponent of this model. He defines a multicongregational church as "one that endorses multiple services and has more than one preaching pastor."[21] He believes this method is a close model to the early church. Hunt notes that "a legitimate model for the New Testament church was to have daily gatherings in both small groups and large."[22] Each Christian did not attend every daily meeting but was probably present at three or four. Hunt also presumes that different pastors preached each week: "Although each pastor may have preached more than once during that time span, this arrangement minimized the fatigue factor for a pastor and other church 'staff' . . . The early church could be described as a multicongregational church — a cluster of congregations, each one separate, yet part of the whole."[23]

Hunt's dream became a reality when Calvary Baptist Church in Las Cruces, New Mexico, where he is associate pastor, developed the multicongregational model. By 1993, Calvary Baptist had expanded to six services, five of them in one location. Their schedule was as follows:[24]

| Saturday | 6:00 P.M. | Contemporary Worship |
| | 7:15 P.M. | Bible Study |
| Sunday | 7:15 A.M. | Early-Bird Bible Study |
| | 8:30 A.M. | Traditional Worship |
| | | Bible Study |
| | 9:30 A.M. | Satellite Service (movie theater) |
| | 9:45 A.M. | Contemporary Worship |
| | | Bible Study |
| | 11:00 A.M. | Traditional Worship |
| | | Bible Study |
| | 6:00 P.M. | Believers' Worship |

## 6. Multicampus

This model is slightly different from the satellite approach. Multicampus refers to one church in more than one location. Unlike the satellite model, the multicampus model has one membership roll, one budget, and one staff. The two more well-known examples of this model are Mt. Paran Church of God in Atlanta, Paul Walker, pastor; and The Church of the Way in Van Nuys, California, Jack Hayford, pastor.

## 7. Sodality Models

In the church-planting models previously described, the institution planting new churches was a local church. In the sodality model of church planting, some agency other than a local church starts the new church. That agency could be a denominational agency, a parachurch organization, or it could refer to the starting of churches by individuals.

## Church Planting: Evangelistic Harvest in the Twenty-First Century

One of the commonly accepted principles of church growth is that new units grow faster and tend to be more evangelistic than existing units. This principle applies to new Sunday School classes, new small groups, new choirs, and new churches.

The new church has not had the opportunity to become inwardly focused. The people still have before them the vision and the mandate for the church's conception: to reach their community for Christ. The new church has not developed institutional inertia, when programs and policies achieve priority over people and purposes. The very newness of the church engenders excitement. And the people never say, "We've never done it that way before," because they never did anything any way before.

The newly-planted church will focus the large portion of its resources on outreach and evangelism. The new converts themselves will evangelize others with enthusiasm. All other factors being equal, the new church has a tremendous evangelistic advantage over the existing church.

Over the past fifty years we have seen the American church become as institutionalized as any point in the nation's history. As society changed dramatically, many churches became ecclesiastical fortresses, doing whatever they could to keep the evil world from penetrating their comfort and tradition.

But a fortress not only keeps outsiders out, it keeps insiders in. The American church is as inwardly focused today as any point in its history. The winds of change, however, are blowing. One by one, traditional churches are going out into the world, leaving the comfort and security of their fortresses behind. In the twenty-first century, more church people will leave their gospel ghetto to do something great for God. They will plant new churches by the tens of thousands. And they will remember that the essence of the Great Commission is not "come to my church." Rather it is "therefore go." Watch for millions to obediently do so.

# Chapter 9

# "Worship the Lord with Gladness . . ."
# Church Trend 9: The Acceptance of
# Multiple Worship Styles

At the crossroads on the path that leads to the future, tradition has placed against each of us ten thousand men to guard the past.

—Belgian philosopher Maurice Maeterlinck

I move that we use the hymnals more in worship services or else get a new pastor who will lead us in the right direction.

—Motion made by member of a Tennessee Baptist church
at the church's monthly business meeting

ROGER ALBRIGHT IS THE MINISTER of music at Amelia Avenue Baptist Church. Next to the pastor of the church, he receives more "input" from members on how he should carry out his job. On this particularly dismal Monday morning, Roger meets with pastor Duane Warren about making major changes in the single Sunday morning worship service. Roger thinks that the dark clouds and the torrential downpour are omens of the days ahead.

"Roger," says Duane, "the time has come. We've prepared the people for this possibility for months. We cannot delay making changes any longer."

"I understand your sentiments, Duane," the worried minister of music responds. "But I think you're headed for trouble. Look, I've been at Amelia Avenue for eleven years; you've just completed your first year. I know these people, particularly the middle and older group. There will be a lynch mob after you if you mess with *their* worship service."

"But Roger," says the pastor, "You've heard from the younger adults. That's where all of our growth is coming from. Many of them are ready to pack up and go to Springmeadow Church unless our service changes. Do you remember what Frank Grigsby told the older deacons in the last deacon's meeting? He called our special music 'dirge anthems' and our hymn selection 'half-notes in hell.' They are running out of patience, Roger."

Roger Albright sighs a breath of inevitability and then speaks, "Okay Duane. I'll follow your leadership. Just understand that you will be offending the big givers in the church. I've lasted this long at this church by not making too many waves. I sure would like to see you celebrate your second anniversary here."

The two men are the only full-time staff members at Amelia Avenue. The other ministries of the 275-attendance church are led by laity or part-time ministers from the local Christian college. The responsibility for instituting such major change rests on the shoulders of Roger and Duane.

From the younger adults' perspective, the proposed changes will be mild. Many of the older adults, however, will feel like their world has been turned upside down. Too many church leaders today see this predicament as a lose-lose situation for similar reasons.

Duane and Roger carefully make plans, asking God for wisdom and guidance. They will not eliminate hymns or hymnals, but they will include the words in the worship bulletin. Praise choruses will follow an upbeat call to worship. Special music, solos, and anthems will include a variety of traditional and contemporary music. A drama team will begin work to include a dramatic presentation once a month.

The two men have worked out one form of a "blended" worship, a mix of both traditional and contemporary elements. In some cases churches adjust well to such incremental change. In other cases any change in style borders on heresy. It is the latter that Roger Albright fears.

Amelia Avenue Baptist Church implements the new worship style with grace and dignity. Some of the younger adults complain because the service is not fully contemporary, but as Roger feared, the older group expresses the most disdain for the changes.

The litany of complaints from the traditionalists include: 1) the music sounds like rock 'n' roll; 2) the hymnals are not used enough; 3) the words that are printed in the bulletin have no music to read with them; 4) drama has no place in a worship service; 5) the dignity is gone from the worship service; 6) the role of the choir is minimized with new soloists and praise teams; 7) the church is compromising with the world; 8) the new music is shallow and plays on the emotions; 9) the order to the worship service is wrong or changeing too much; and 10) what was wrong with the old way?

Duane Warren remembers his colleague's words. Now he too prays that he will celebrate a second anniversary at the church.

## Worship or Entertainment? Compromise or Renewal?

I have pastored four churches ranging in size from one hundred to nearly two thousand. These four churches were in four different states above and below the Mason-Dixon line. One church was as rural as rural gets. Another was in a blue-collar community near a major city. A third was in a resort community right on the beautiful white sands of the Gulf of Mexico. The fourth was in an affluent suburb of the largest city in the state. Four significantly different churches in dramatically different locations. Yet all four churches had one noticeable similarity: tampering with the worship service was grounds for capital punishment.

Why are Christians so sensitive about the style and music of worship services? For many believers, the worship service *is* the church. They go to Sunday School and then go to *church* (worship service). Thus a change in the service is more than a stylistic adjustment; it is a desecration of holy ground.

For others the worship service is a heritage, a tradition that evokes warm memories and hopeful tommorrows. Any significant change is difficult because of the rich heritage in every known hymn, doxology, and order of service. And that heritage is an oasis in the cultural desert that exists beyond the church walls.

The issue for others is change. They cannot control the rapid changes in technology, science, education, business, entertainment, or politics. The church offers stability and certainty in the midst of the nation's instability and uncertainty.

Finally, some believers fiercely contend that changes in worship reflect the church's compromise with the world. We are called to be salt and light, set apart from the world's values. Why should we imitate the world in the very act of worshiping the separated and holy God?

In this chapter we will examine the changes taking place in worship services in our nation. But before we proceed, we will state the emerging trend: A variety of worship styles will be the norm in traditional churches in America. Over the past four decades, the "label" of a church was most often associated with the style of worship. A contemporary church, had a contemporary worship service, and a traditional church had a traditional worship service.

However, the twenty-first century church will not be labeled or defined by its style of worship. Traditional churches will have a variety of worship styles. As we stated in the introductory chapter, the word "traditional" will mean that a church is intentionally communicating through the generations the unchanging truth of the Christian faith while building a sense of family and community. Traditional will mean that a church sees its apostolic heritage as true tradition—not a particular style of worship. Tradition will mean "thoroughly biblical," with a passion for teaching and communicating the truths of Scripture. The whole counsel of God as revealed in the Bible will be taught and preached in the twenty-first century traditional church.

Yet for many the question still remains: Is a shift to a culturally-palatable worship style healthy or heretical? Perhaps a historical look at worship styles over the past two thousand years will help us get a broader perspective. Such a journey may also give us a clue as to what our future holds.

## Worship through the Ages

Our word *worship* comes from the Anglo-Saxon *weorthscipe* that eventually became *worthsip* and finally *worship*. Worship is thus "the act of giving honor and glory to someone of worth." When we worship God we ascribe to Him worth that He alone is worthy to receive.[1]

Public or corporate worship services have been an essential activity of the gathered church since Pentecost. Excitement and devotion to Christ was evident in the earliest Christian worship services: "Every day they continued to meet together in the temple courts. They broke bread in their homes and ate together with glad an sincere hearts, praising God and enjoying the favor of all the people. And the Lord added to their number daily those who were being saved" (Acts 2:46–47).

### The Early and Medieval Church in Worship

The most ancient Christian hymnwriters sought to communicate biblical truths through worship to a culture largely influenced by pagan Greek practices.[2] Since the Gnostics and Arians of the second century were reaching a wide public audience with their hymns of heretical teachings, Christian writers sought to counter them with hymns of orthodoxy. But the Christians did not develop their own style; they opted to use the popular style of the Gnostics.

Steve Miller notes that the works of an early hymn writer, "Ephraem Syrus (307–373), a distinguished father of the Syrian church, countered by writing hymns to champion orthodoxy. But rather than create a new, sacred style in which to couch the truth, he opted to use the same meters as popular Gnostic songs and thus exerted a powerful influence."[3]

Interestingly, then, the early church was influenced, at least in the musical aspect of worship, by sources which were both pagan and heretical. Although the words to the music never compromised biblical truths, they were placed in the tune and meters of songs that had popular but pagan origins. During these early years the church continued to borrow secular musical scores and practices.[4]

Thus worship and musical style continued without significant change until the sixth century. It was then that Pope Gregory the Great modified the scales and developed what is now known as the Gregorian chant.[5] "All voices sang in unison, all musical instruments were restricted, and only men were allowed to sing in worship."[6]

No single style of music has dominated Christian worship for so long a period as the Gregorian chant. For almost a full millennium the chant was not only accepted but, for the most part, mandated by the leadership of the church. Pope John XII (c. 1324) issued a decree that rejected "any means of composition which expressed contemporary secular art."[7]

The medieval church made a clear distinction between "sacred" and "secular" music. The world's popular music was not heard in the church's worship services. The chant continued to be the style of reverence while anything else was secular and unacceptable. This trend continued unabated until the late fifteenth century when many Germans were converted to Catholicism.

The Germans were hearty and avid singers. The common person in Germany knew hundreds of songs, many of which had their origins in the praise of heathen deities.[8] After these Germans became Christians, they naturally began composing their own hymns with religious lyrics and the old familiar, secular tunes. They even took the staid Latin hymns of the Roman church and translated the words into the language of the common people, while adding the tunes of the culture.

By 1504 the Mohemians, Moravians, and followers of John Huss published a hymnbook that included the popular praise songs.[9] At least in one geographical area, the music and worship was breaking away from the mold of high formality and Gregorian chants. But the Roman Catholic Church did not bless the actions of these musical renegades. Though the German Christian worship did not spread significantly in Christendom during the early sixteenth century, it did plant seeds for change that would blossom in a period called the Reformation under the leadership of a man named Martin Luther.

### Worship And The Reformation

For theologians, the Reformation means Martin Luther's "Ninety-five Theses" at Wittenberg, justification by faith, the singular authority of Scripture, and a new interest and zeal for biblical theology. But for Luther and other reformers, there was also a great passion to reform the worship of the church. Roman Catholicism, contended Luther, had not only taken the Bible out of the hands of the common person, but it had also removed any sense of true and understandable worship.

Martin Luther could not understand why the secular world had "so many beautiful songs, while in the religious field we have such rotten, lifeless stuff."[10] He understood that the average German would not fully appreciate the majesty of Christian music unless it was according to their own preferences and culture. Luther decided to place biblical words in culturally-popular tunes. After all, he surmised, "the devil has no need of all the good tunes for himself."[11]

Luther's great desire was for music to communicate biblical truths that would engender a passion for the Savior. His hopes were exceeded by the impact of his own music. One church historian noted that Luther's hymns "were carried from place to place in the form of leaflets, or were sung in towns and villages by wandering minstrels. Memorized by young and old throughout Germany, they paved the way for the Reformation."[12]

Thirty-six hymns have been credited to Luther, including "A Mighty Fortress Is Our God." His music, and the music of others who adopted his culturally-popular style, spread like wildfire in homes, in workplaces, in the cities, and on the farms. The impact of his music was noted even by these who opposed Luther. Jesuit Adam Conzenius bemoaned the influence of Luther's music: "Luther's hymns have destroyed more souls than his writings and speeches."[13]

Not all of his fellow reformers agreed with Luther's perceived capitulation to culture. John Calvin was the best known of the critics. He believed that instruments were only tolerated in the Old Testament because of the spiritual immaturity of Israel. He also opposed any lyrics not found in Scripture. The Psalms, Calvin contended, are the only true inspired words to be sung in the context of worship.

Though Luther's influence initially was more extensive than Calvin's, the impact of Calvin was nevertheless significant. In 1562, a complete edition of the musical Psalms was published in the *Geneva Psalter*.[14] The volume was translated into several languages and received with enthusiasm in parts of France, Switzerland, Germany, Holland, and Denmark.[15] Though Calvin's works were limited to the words of Scripture, and though singing in parts and using instruments were prohibited, he nevertheless used the tunes of the secular world. As the church moved into the seventeenth century, two broad forms of sacred music were advocated: Luther's influence of singing hymns and Calvin's advocacy of psalm singing.

### The Age of Hymnody

As the years progressed, Calvin's psalm singing gained favor over Luther's hymns. Germany continued mostly in Luther's traditions while Protestants in England and Scotland were mostly advocates of psalm singing.[16] Attempts to introduce hymns in psalm-singing churches often resulted in fierce opposition. John Bunyan's attempt to introduce hymns in his own church resulted in a great controversy and, ultimately, a church split. After his death the church compromised by allowing those in opposition to hymns to sit in silence or to go to the vestibule and wait until the hymn singing concluded.[17]

Psalm singing became more awkward as the Christians of the late seventeenth century developed an appreciation for the fine literature, poetry, and music of their day. Steve Miller explains: "In part, the problem was inherent in the nature of the metrical psalm. When the biblical psalm was forced into rhyme and meter, while strictly adhering to the content of the original psalm, the resulting poetry was often awkward."[18]

Isaac Watts, in many respects the father of the modern hymn, was also uncomfortable with the Christian music of his day. He certainly was knowledgeable of the literature of his era. Watts was proficient in Latin at age four, Greek at nine, French at ten, and Hebrew at thirteen.[19] His first challenge to the scared music style was the hymn, "Behold the Glories of the Lamb," composed at age twenty.[20] Isaac Watts eventually wrote 750 hymns, including the cherished

"O God, Our Help in Ages Past," "Joy to the World!" "Alas? and Did My Savior Bleed?" and "When I Survey the Wondrous Cross."[21]

Miller explains Watts' philosophy: "His desire was to harness and use the appeal of good poetry. Instead of producing ornate songs for the literary sophisticate, he sought to produce songs for the edification of the simplest worshiper."[22] But Watts' noble efforts did not succeed without intense opposition. One source came from those who thought poetry was the art form of the world and Satan. They did not claim that Watts' poetry was evil, but that it was a tool that had been associated with evil. Guilt by association was sufficient reason to protest.

Another source of opposition came from those who felt that Watts' music was unbiblical since it did not quote Scripture verbatim. For example, William Romaine asked in 1755: "Why should Watts, or any hymnmaker, not only take the precedence of the Holy Ghost, but also thrust him entirely out of the church?"[23]

But the momentum and acceptance of Watts' hymnody could not be stopped. Sometimes churches split and sometimes pastors were fired (sound familiar?), but acceptance continued. By the mid-eighteenth century, many churches were singing hymns and were fiercely defending them as the "right traditions."

Other well-known advocates of hymnody helped carry the momentum through two centuries. In the eighteenth century Charles Wesley and his brother John wanted to rid the church of cold formality and advocated an exciting and vibrant relationship with the living Christ. Charles Wesley wrote an unbelievable six thousand hymns including "Hark! The Herald Angels Sing," and "Love Divine, All Loves Excelling."[24] He, too, was also accused of worldly compromise because he used styles and folk tunes of his day. But the momentum would not be stopped.

A divine acceleration of hymnody took place with the First and Second Great Awakenings. By the time of the camp meetings of the Second Awakening, the music was moving faster with a more upbeat tempo. The rural Baptists and others "wanted music that would set their hands to clapping, their feet to tapping, and their bodies to swaying."[25] From these fires of revival at least two branches of hymnody were born: gospel songs and Negro spirituals.

This new hymnody set the stage for the nineteenth century revival music of Ira Sankey, the musician whose partnership with the great evangelist D. L. Moody is legend. Moody believed that music played a critical role in the revival meetings he led. He sought God's anointed person for the task.

Miller tells how Moody chose Ira Sankey: "In seeking to use music in his campaigns, Moody felt that something new was needed. In his estimation, the camp meeting songs would not be appropriate for the big city masses. Upon hearing the song leading of Ira Sankey in 1870, Moody knew he had found the man and the style."[26]

But Ira Sankey was not the choice of many fellow musicians. Miller continues: "Trained musicians did not esteem Sankey as an accomplished singer, but he never claimed to be one. He was not seeking to impress serious musicians, but rather to reach the masses with the gospel. His voice and manner had the ability to stir hearts, draw people's attention to the words and plant a melody within the listener."[27]

Sankey's style was popular rather than classical. And that style appealed to the masses. One Edinburgh woman wrote, "Mr. Sankey sings with the conviction that souls are receiving Jesus between one note and the next."[28]

While the music of Sankey was reaching the masses on the American frontier, William Booth and the Salvation Army were producing music that was touching the common people of England. The use of a large variety of instruments gave a new twist to a hymnody that had gained wide acceptance at the end of the nineteenth century.

The beginning of the twentieth century saw the debate over the value of hymnody close. Of course, there were minor debates over the *style* of hymnody: classical hymns, gospel songs, Negro spirituals, revival hymns, or hymns with multiple instrumentation. But the hymn had found its place of acceptance as the Gregorian chant once had and as the psalm singing once had. It would not be challenged for more than half a century, when a new and radically-perceived music began to irritate all but the younger generations: contemporary Christian music.

## The Christian Music Debate . . . Again!

Christians have always shown strong emotions about their worship and musical preferences. One author makes clear his position on contemporary Christian music: "I view this integration of rock music and the worship of God as clear evidence that the church has entered the final Laodicean age of apostasy."[29]

But critics can be found on both sides. Another concerned author speaks against more formal worship styles with equal intensity: "Let's set the record straight for a minute. There are no great, vibrant, soul-winning churches reaching great numbers of people, baptizing hundreds of converts, reaching the masses that have stiff music, sevenfold amens, and a steady diet of classical anthems. None. That's not a few. That's none, none, none."[30]

What are some criticisms of contemporary Christian music? Below are but a few that some opponents have mentioned:

- Christian rock music is harmful to both the mind and the body.

- Contemporary Christian music demonstrates a compromise with the world's culture when Christ has called us to be salt and light in the world (Matt. 5:13–16).

- The beat of Christian rock music is the same kind of beat used by African tribes to call upon demons.

- The music of the sixties used in a Christian context devalues the majesty and holiness of God.

- Contemporary Christian music leads to immoral lifestyles.

- That music is just too doggone loud!

### Learning Lessons from Our Past and Our Future

The attacks on contemporary Christian music are nothing new in the history of Christian worship. Perhaps the precise details of the complaints are different, but the essence of the opposition is still the same. The lessons we learn from history help us evaluate the current climate for worship. We can also look to the trends of the future to get some idea about the type of worship styles we will see in the twenty-first century Christian church.

### Lessons from Our Past

The several pages written earlier in this chapter were more than an exercise in historical remembrances. They were written to demonstrate that music styles have changed in the past, and we can expect more changes in the future. And, with each shift in musical style, we can expect intense opposition and words of hyperbole.

In terms of music, the organ was initially rejected by the Catholic church which remembered that the early organ accompanied the slaughter of Christians in the Roman era.[31] It was later rejected by the reformers who associated it with the Catholic church.[32] The city of Zurich banned the organ from both civic and church functions in 1524.[33]

Many Christians of the Middle Ages claimed that the augmented four chord was demonically possessed.[34] Later, thirds and sixths were banned in some settings because they were deemed sensual. Even later "the syncopated beat was rejected because of its association with the ragtime era, but hymns like 'Since Jesus Came Into My Heart' survived the initial shock of many skeptical worshipers and today are considered traditional hymns."[35]

Most nineteenth century churches rejected the piano because of its association with the secular world.[36] And the eighteenth-century Moravians rejected the violin because it was associated with the dancing of the devil.[37] Early in this century, as the liturgical movement gained its own momentum, the solo was banned since it glorified the singer.[38] And while most churches today accept soloists, many reject applause for them for the same reason that the soloists were originally rejected — personal glorification.

Steve Miller[ ] notes that church history demonstrates a clear cyclical pattern for worship and music.[39] The first stage is called *separation*, where the worship style in the church communicates only to the firmly-entrenched church members. Those outside the church do not identify at all with the old forms of music.

The second stage is *integration*, where innovators adopt the musical style of the culture in order to reach that culture. That stage is quickly followed by *conflict*, the opposition of the unbending traditionalists.

Fourth, the music of the people becomes a new and powerful communication and outreach tool of the church. This stage is called *renewal* as worship is once again in the language of the people.

Finally, the new worship style becomes accepted as a tradition unto itself. This stage is called *entrenchment*, which will return to the first stage unless the church maintains a continuous missions mindset.

Almost without exception, churches that moved out of the separation stage did so with a missionary motive. They knew their present style of worship was not reaching the masses. Therefore they listened to the music of the common people and adapted their worship style to reach unbelievers. They followed the path of contextualization that Paul urges in his letter to the church at Corinth: "I have become all things to all men so that by all possible means I might save some. I do all this for the sake of the gospel, that I may share in its blessings" (1 Cor. 9:22–23).

Eventually the worship style that was initiated with a missionary motive becomes the accepted style of the believers. And quite often during these times, the church experiences a great evangelistic harvest.

## Lessons from Our Future

While the past teaches us that worship styles change with different eras, the lessons of the future are somewhat different. Like the past two thousand years, believers will continue to accept new worship styles. But the twenty-first century worship service in America will have as much variety as there are cultures and preferences in the nation.

For most of church history, variety has only existed within a type of worship style or music, for example different styles within hymnody. But as this century and millennium comes to a close, one might expect a traditional hymn worship church, a country gospel church, and a contemporary worship church all in the same community. With the advent of television and instantaneous communication, the world is getting smaller. And as the world gets smaller, greater tolerance for diverse cultures will mean greater tolerance for diverse worship styles.

Similarly, more frequent and less expensive world travel will mean that more Christians in America will have the opportunity to experience the diversity of worship styles around the globe. Believers will then return to America with a greater appreciation for the influence of culture on their own worship styles. One Southern Baptist church member from Alabama returned from Nigeria with a new "tolerance" for some of the worship approaches she had firmly opposed in her own church. She learned that worship styles are not monolithic, but vary considerably from culture to culture, even within the preferences of one local church.

Training for the church worship and music ministry also reflects this growing acceptance of multiple worship styles. When Lloyd Mims was named dean of the School of Church Music at The Southern Baptist Theological Seminary in 1994, he made a commitment to prepare men and women for the diverse worship approaches in our denomination. Twenty years ago one could attend a Southern Baptist church at almost any place in our nation and know with a high degree of accuracy what type of worship to expect. Today such homogeneity no longer exists. One community may have three Southern Baptist churches with three different worship styles within a few miles of one another.

The chapel services at my seminary likewise reflect this diversity. The style of worship alternates between liturgical, traditional, blended, and contemporary. And I must admit it is somewhat interesting to watch our professors interact with the contemporary Christian bands we "import" every fourth service!

In our first chapel service with this alternative format, Professor Don Hustad spoke to our seminary community about our own response to the new worship services. He asked the rhetorical question: "How do we worship this God who is beyond all our imagining, yet closer than hands and feet?" Dr. Hustad's answer touched me deeply as he spoke of the multiple expressions of worship. "With the spirit and with the understanding also . . . congnitive and intuitive, rational and emotional — using words that stretch our minds and stimulate our imaginations, and with simple prayers deep in our hearts. With organs, as well as guitars and synthesizers . . . with great anthems and hymns, as well as with gospel songs, scripture choruses, and contemporary music. With silence as well as with sound. With planned order, and also with spontaneity!"[40]

A recent article on worship diversity reflects the paradigm shift in thinking about the topic among Southern Baptists. Trennis Henderson notes·that "'typical' Baptist worship services vary from a rural congregation with a simple format of singing, praying, and preaching to a suburban megachurch that highlights praise choruses and 'seeker' services."[41] Henderson comments that the only certainty about Southern Baptist worship services today is their diversity: "On any given Sunday, worship elements may range from a denim-clad song leader strumming a guitar to a formal liturgical service complete with an orchestra and a robed minister. Worship settings run the gamut from tiny one-room church houses perched on the end of dirt roads to plush, state-of-the-art worship centers in prime locations near bustling freeways."[42]

A few years ago the pundits were forecasting a shift to contemporary worship as the worship style of the twenty-first century. Today we can only say that contemporary worship will be one of many approaches. Perhaps even more amazing will be the low level of conflict compared to past centuries. The typical American churchgoer will have a much greater tolerance for worship styles that are contrary to his or her preference.

What will be the prominent worship styles of the next century? Likely, some will develop that we could not even perceive today. But at least five major approaches to worship will be advocated at the beginning of the century.

## Worship Styles at the Beginning of the Twenty-first Century

With only a few years remaining in this century, we can say with some degree of confidence that four major styles of worship will still be practiced in the year 2000. These four do not represent an exhaustive listing, nor do they consider the wide variety of approaches within each category.

### Traditional Worship

Well-known hymns are the mainstay of today's traditional worship services. This love of hymns means that standard hymns such as "Great is Thy Faithfulness" or "Amazing Grace" are sung with enthusiasm and familiarity. "Elements such as a prelude, greeting, invocation, hymns, announcements, offering, choir special, Scripture reading, sermon, and invitation are arranged in a certain sequence that varies little from week to week. The traditional model may appear in different churches of various sizes."[43]

Some churches may include a long pastoral prayer, the recitation of the Apostles' Creed, or responsive readings. The key is that the service has a degree of informality within a well-established pattern and structure. The organ and the piano are the typical instruments of choice.

### Contemporary Worship

The very name "contemporary" means that something new or modern is inherent in the service. Certainly most of the music is of more recent composition than most hymns. Much of the music in contemporary services is not found in hymnals, but is projected on a large screen or written on a song sheet. The types of instruments used vary greatly, though many contemporary churches take advantage of the versatility of an electronic keyboard.

The minister of music or worship leader or director of worship and music plays a role with a profile almost as high as the pastor/preacher. He or she leads not only with singing, but by speaking during the worship service, often preceding songs and choruses.

Drama is an element that has become common in many contemporary churches. The dramatic presentation is typically tied to a central theme that is also reflected in the sermon. And the preached message itself tends to be high-application spoken in a conversational manner.

Most contemporary churches have an intentional "seeker-sensitive" approach. Seekers are unbelievers who are visiting the worship services. Care is taken to make certain that the seekers can follow everything that is said and done in the service. A mindset exists that asks the question: "How would I feel if I was an unbeliever and came to this worship service for the first time?" Sometimes the traditional invitation is eliminated for this very reason. And the offering is usually taken with the disclaimer that guests are not expected to give. The seekers are allowed to keep their anonymity. At no point in the service are the members and non-members identified separately, such as asking visitors to remain seated while the members stand. Seeker sensitivity thus frames most of the elements of contemporary services.

## Blended Worship

As I have visited churches across our nation, I have found the blended format to be growing rapidly in acceptance. "Blended" typically refers to the combination of elements from the traditional and contemporary styles. How different churches "blend" the two styles depends on each church.

The central thrust of the blended service is to retain the music of traditional hymnody while introducing new music and approaches. The context and history of the church usually determine the pace by which new elements are introduced and the balance between contemporary and traditional elements.

When I was pastor of Green Valley Baptist Church in Birmingham, we consciously developed a blended worship style. The balance in our services, however, favored the traditional elements. We had hymns and hymnbooks, choirs, an orchestra, and a fairly-predictable order of worship. But we also had choruses printed in the worship bulletin, the offering at the end of the service (that is really radical in some churches!), explanations of elements that may seem foreign to a seeker, and the intentionality of not recognizing guests.

Yet I have been in other churches where one of two well-known hymns are included as the *only* elements of traditional worship. Otherwise the service seems very contemporary. In the strictest sense this type of service is also blended, although it would be significantly different from the service described above.

Some predict that blended worship is a transitional style, here only for a season as most churches become contemporary. To the contrary, the blended worship style is developing its own identity and proponents. Many of the middle and younger adult generations appreciate both hymns and contemporary Christian music. They also appreciate both the anonymity allowed in contemporary services and the sense of order and familiarity of traditional services. They like choirs and praise ensembles, hymnals and overhead screens with choruses projected on it.

The blended service may have begun as a transitional style, but it has become the style of choice in many regions. Look for the blended service to gain acceptance for at least the next twenty years.

## Liturgical Worship

Advocates of liturgical worship object to the criticism that their style of worship is cold or impersonal. Formality is not synonymous with lack of warmth. Says one pastor of a liturgical church, "We're warm, human, caring — but with dignity."[44]

Liturgical worship generally follows a prescribed order that includes such elements as printed readings or prayers, silence, stately hymns, Old Testament and New Testament readings (some include the Psalms), and a sermon that is often based on a text suggested by the Revised Common Lectionary.

Often visual symbols help define the worship setting. The use of banners, candles, and stained-glass windows are not uncommon in many liturgical services. The ministers may add to this visual effect by wearing liturgical robes.

Liturgical worship is common in Roman Catholicism, mainline Protestant denominations such as Lutherans and Episcopalians, and even in a relatively small but significant number of Baptist churches. These churches often follow the liturgical calendar as much as possible, with particular emphases on the Advent and Lenten seasons.

Those who attend liturgical worship services often speak of its dignity and quietness which contrasts dramatically with the hectic pace of the world outside the walls of the church building. With the frantic and busy lifestyles of most Americans, the liturgical worship offers a time of quietness and reflection, a time to think, rest, and pray. One pastor of a liturgical church comments: "There needs to be a place for some people to be quiet. We have a lot of quietness built into our services. That's planned — it's intentional."[45]

The future of the liturgical church deserves two comments. First, a relatively small but still significant number of churches will continue to adopt this worship style. It is not a dying form of worship;

it is simply the choice of a smaller number of churchgoers than other styles. Nevertheless, liturgical worship will continue to have its place in American worship. Second, the liturgical movement may actually experience a modest growth in the next century. As acceptance of all worship styles grow, some churchgoers will feel a greater freedom to attend a worship service that their peers once called dull, dry, and cold. Liturgical need not be any of those adjectives. It offers a time of quietness and dignity, and such will be the choice of many in the next century.

## Other Worship Styles

Four worship styles only begin to describe the variety that now exists in America. These styles also are not necessarily reflective of the worship practices of African-American and ethnic churches in America. For example, here is one description of a Baptist African-American church: "Joyful Baptists participate in celebrative worship in the African-American tradition. Through verbal responses such as "Amen," "That's right," and "Preach it," worshipers affirm the message of the pastor and musician. Frequently, when led by the Holy Spirit, they testify about God's work in their lives. Services commonly are two hours or more in length. The warmth and fellowship among worshipers balances powerful, dynamic preaching."[46]

## Worship in the Twenty-first Century: New Paradigms for a New Millennium

The only fully predictable element of twenty-first century worship will be its unpredictability. A new paradigm exists in the minds of worshipers that accepts multiple worship styles. This paradigm is different than that of previous centuries. In years past worship was largely monolithic. To depart from the accepted style was often seen as heretical or doctrinal deviation. Indeed for many such a shift *was* doctrinal deviation.

Churchgoers of the twenty-first century will continue to have their own preferences of worship styles. But they will no longer consider other styles as deviant or inferior. A new openness is emerging that will allow more energy for true worship rather than needless debate. And in different styles, languages, music, and messages, Christians from all points of the globe will ascribe worthiness to the only One who is truly worthy.

I will sing of the love of the LORD forever;
with my mouth I will make your
faithfulness known through all generations.
I will declare that your love stands
firm forever,
that you established your faithfulness
in heaven itself.
(Psalm 89:1–2)

# Chapter 10

# "Wonders and Miraculous Signs . . ." Lessons for the Local Church

Remember, buddy, God is in control. He will still be with you after I'm gone.

—Sam S. Rainer, Sr., my father,
speaking to me four
days before his death

W HEN MY FATHER DIED I, perhaps for the first time, wondered if my world was falling apart. In retrospect, I realize that I placed my dad on a very high pedestal. No one is as perfect as I perceived him to be. Nevertheless, a good man, a very good man, had slipped from this life into eternal life. I was crushed.

The most surprising emotion I recall was that of anger toward God. I felt guilty for feeling angry, but I kept sensing that God had lost control of this world by allowing my father to die at the relatively young age of 62.

But God's grace soon became evident in the most unusual ways. Foremost was the new appreciation and deepened love I gained for my mother and my older brother, my only sibling. Though I had always admired both of them, I now saw them in a new and revealing light.

In Mama I saw a strength and dignity that could not be explained in natural terms. She handled her grief as only one with supernatural strength could manage. Her devotion to Dad had been unsurpassed in all the wives of husbands I had ever known. Yet there was Mama—clothed with dignity and love and concern for others. I was humbled by God's power so evident in one I loved so dearly.

My brother, Sam, Jr., had always been a caring big brother to me. Growing up as both the younger and wilder sibling, I turned to him often for help and deliverance from the many messes in which I found myself. And Sam was always there, never judgmental, just there for his little brother.

But after Dad's death I saw him with eyes that had not been previously opened. I saw Sam, Jr. as the worthy namesake of Sam, Sr., because I saw so much of Dad in him. There was that quiet strength, that ability to find good in others, that warm sense of humor, and that Christlike quality of always putting others before himself.

Several months after Dad's death, I reflected on these two loved ones in a moment of quiet. I began praising God for them and then I paused. It occurred to me that my attitude toward God had taken a dramatic shift—from anger to praise. And it also made me wonder how I ever doubted that God was in control. And on that early morning in late December, I lifted my voice up again in praise to the sovereign God who loves me unconditionally.

## Trend Predictions . . .with Caution

The sovereignty of God is a theme that frames the whole of Scripture. We worship and serve a God who is in absolute control. Regardless of life's situations, the God of this universe is always in control of the past, present, and future.

The trends that have been presented were written with a humble heart that realizes that God can move in whatever direction He pleases. I am not prophetic in the sense of knowing clearly the future of the church. I have attempted to be an "Issachar," one who listens carefully to the times—past, present, and future—so that we, as the church, may proceed with wisdom and discernment. But infallibility is an attribute that belongs only to God and His Word. It is certainly not a claim for this book.

I also realize that some of these trends contradict those of other church observers. Men and women of higher intellect and stature than I will disagree with some of my conclusions. This book's purpose was not to suggest that other trend predictions are wrong. I respect other points of view, realizing that any error may be my own.

But I believe that any differences of opinion in trends may be the result of methodological differences. For example, one excellent book on Christianity in the twenty-first century based most of its conclusions on emerging developments.[1] The author looked at innovative churches and Christian organizations and projected greater acceptance of the innovations in the years ahead. Such an approach is a worthy manner of study that should get our attention.

Another approach is the survey-research method of discerning the times. Large numbers of people are asked well-prepared questions dealing with a variety of issues. If the same questions are asked over a period of a few years, a discernible trend emerges that can be extended into the future.[2]

The approach that I have taken, like others, is to listen carefully to developments in our present age and to note patterns that become evident. But I have looked at long-term historical developments as well. We can learn vital lessons from our past to help us discern our future.

One example of my approach is that of the great prayer movement. The role of prayer is becoming larger in many churches across our land; that is a present observation. But history reminds us that any time such prayer movements have touched our land, churches have been renewed, methodologies have been evaluated, priorities have changed, and evangelistic growth has resulted. For example, the Prayer Revival of 1857 in the United States resulted in one million conversions over a two-year period.[3] And the Prayer Revival of 1859 in Great Britain also resulted in over one million conversions in two years. (The population of all of Great Britain was only 27 million at that time.)[4] In both of these great prayer movements a significant lay ministry developed and grew. Such has been the case with all prayer movements in church history.[5] Can we not then conclude that the great prayer movement today will soon have similar results?

Another example concerns the related topics of Sunday School renewal and rediscovery of the Bible and theology. One significant study done by and for mainline denominations found that in-depth teaching and preaching of orthodox Christian belief was the single best predictor of church participation.[6] Strong Sunday Schools and scripturally-authoritative preaching engendered long-term health for the church.[7] As this historical reality becomes more apparent, should we not anticipate more churches returning to the basics of preaching and Christian education?

All of these trends point to a new awakening for the traditional church. Such traditional elements as Sunday School, prayer meetings, and expository preaching may be returning with new vigor and health in churches across our land.

Understanding the times in which we live and understanding trends toward the future can be a fun and intellectually-stimulating exercise. But we have gained little unless we ask how such information can help us and our churches. Our sovereign God *is* in total control; that is our assurance and hope. But God does not expect us to be passive participants in His world. He mandates that we go into the world well equipped by learning from the new insights He has revealed to us.

What then are some of the lessons for the local church? How can we use this information to make a difference for the Kingdom? Below are a few suggestions.

## Make Prayer a Priority in Your Church

A layperson recently heard a lecture I gave that included some of the information presented in this book. She was especially moved by the prayer awakening taking place in our land. But she, as a layperson, wondered what she alone could do—particularly if pastoral support was lacking.

I shared with her the fact that the Prayer Revival of 1857 had its origins in the work of Jeremiah C. Lanphier, a layperson in New York City's Fulton Street North Dutch Church. It was his persistence in prayer and his urging others to join him that turned a city and a nation around.[8] God's Word promises us that "the prayer of a righteous man [or woman!] is powerful and effective" (James 5:16). The prayers of one person for awakening and renewal can and will make a difference.

If you are a pastor or other leader in your church, your leadership in prayer can be a powerful force of spiritual renewal. May I suggest some very practical steps in this direction?

### 1. Model Prayer

When your church members talk to you about prayer, or when you preach about prayer, you should be able to speak from your own personal experience. You, as a leader, must model prayer in all that you do and say.

In the last two churches I pastored, we had an understanding that my early-morning hours in the office would be time in prayer. Sometimes I prayed alone; on other days I prayed with staff and laypersons. It was understood that only emergencies could interrupt my prayer time. And only two such emergencies occurred over several years.

One of the joys of my pastoral ministry was to overhear a conversation between two church members that went something like this: "Well we can't have the meeting with the pastor on Tuesday morning because he will be in prayer. Let's find another time to ask him." Remember pastors, the first item in your biblical job description is prayer (Acts 6:4).

## 2. Lead Your Church in a Time of Rediscovering Prayer

Two of the most significant events in my pastoral ministry were directly related to prayer. Early in my ministry at Azalea Baptist Church in St. Petersburg, Florida, we called our church to a time of twenty-four hour prayer. We specifically prayed for renewal in our fellowship. Though our church was not large (average attendance was about 250), we had people in several different rooms in the church praying at every hour of the night and day.

At Green Valley Baptist Church the prayer conference led by Don Miller was a tremendous event. Lives were changed and renewal was evident. Since this conference took place just prior to my move to Southern Seminary, I have been able to share the freshness of that event with my students.

These examples are but two of many ways you can lead your church to rediscover prayer. But a key to the long-term success of any prayer event is the intentional effort to establish some type of ongoing prayer ministry or prayer emphasis. Don Miller shares the concept of an "upper room," an intercessory prayer room to be used on a regular basis. At Green Valley, our upper room was used in one-hour segments of intercessory prayer for almost every daytime hour of the five weekdays.

## Rethink Preaching and Teaching

In many churches we have taken the "dumb down" approach to preaching and teaching the theology of the Bible. Because we have been so concerned with seekers and nominal Christians we have lowered the quality and depth of our preaching and teaching. The people in our churches need to be challenged with the depths of Scripture. They need "meat" rather than "milk" week after week. The apostle Paul chastised the Corinthian Christians because they were not ready for "solid food." They were only taking milk because they were "worldly . . .[with] jealousy and quarreling among you" (1 Cor. 3:1–3).

But our churches need more depth in biblical teaching and preaching. Special arrangements and classes should be made for new Christians and persons who are not prepared for in-depth teachings. But the church as a whole needs strong doctrinal teaching on a consistent basis. I believe this is precisely what Paul had in mind when he told Timothy: "Preach the Word; be prepared in season and out of season; correct, rebuke and encourage—with great patience and careful instruction. For the time will come when men will not put up with *sound doctrine*. Instead, to suit their own desires, they will gather around them a great number of teachers to say what their itching ears want to hear" (2 Tim. 4:2–3, emphasis added).

The strong and vibrant churches twenty years from today will be those churches that laid a solid foundation of deep biblical teachings. We have lowered the expectations of the people in our churches, and many people have responded with an apathy for God's Word. By raising expectations we will raise the level of learning in our churches and educate a new generation in the truths of the Bible.

## Give Sunday School a Very High Priority

Mainline denominations are now discovering the effect of years of de-emphasizing Sunday Schools. I repeat a quote from the Hoge study cited in chapter 3. Speaking of the necessity of communicating biblical truths to every successive generation, the study said: "Unless the youth are firmly socialized into its [the Bible's] tenets and standards, the strength of the religious community will eventually ebb away."[9]

Worship services have received considerable attention during the past few years. The renewal of worship in America has been healthy for our churches. New life has come into many churches because of the considerable amount of energy that has gone into planning and praying over each week's services. Unfortunately, the refocus on worship has sometimes taken place at the expense of Sunday School. A new priority must be given to Sunday School.

In single-staff churches, the pastor and a key layperson must devote much of their time to the Sunday School organization. Multiple-staff churches should see the minister of education (or similarly-named position) as a key player in the organization. The Sunday School classes must have the best teachers with an ongoing process of teacher training and development. The Sunday School teacher should be a highly-committed person upon whom high expectations are placed. Though many of our church leaders would hesitate to admit it, some of our Sunday School teachers today are ill-equipped, unprepared, and consistently tardy. We are forsaking present and future generations by accepting shoddy and uncaring work in our Sunday School leadership.

The Sunday School should also view itself as a key outreach arm of the church. Though the "front door" has shifted somewhat to worship, the real key to bringing people into the church and ultimately to the Savior is the development of relationships with unbelievers. When new Sunday School classes are started with a mandate to grow, members in that class begin thinking about that lost co-worker or that unsaved neighbor. Sunday School *can* return to a position of outreach ministry if relationships are emphasized *and* if classes are expected to reproduce themselves.

The renewal of the Sunday School gives the new and renewed denominations of the twenty-first century the opportunity to make an impact with challenging Bible study material. Though material should be available for new Christians and others needing very basic studies, most Christians will need to be challenged with intense Bible study curriculum. And church leaders will need to raise the expectations of the members to study and grasp the material.

My sons attend an excellent school where many teachers have high expectations for the students. My boys have performed better, shown more enthusiasm, and demonstrated higher motivation in those classes where the expectations were higher and the studies more difficult. We know this principle works for our children. Why are we not challenging our adults in the study of the most important material in the universe—God's Holy Bible?

Many church members today are attending non-church and parachurch Bible studies because Sunday School became too superficial and elementary for them. Wise church leaders of the twenty-first century will "bring the Bible back" to the local church, where it will be studied with enthusiasm and intensity.

### Create an Atmosphere for Laity-led Ministries

I recently met with a most unusual man. He was talking with me about entering Southern Seminary. Yet he was significantly different than other prospective students with whom I have met. This man had a very impressive resume. He had been involved in countless ministries in both his local church and in numerous locations around the world. But he had done all this ministry while working full-time as a high-level executive for NASA. Now he is in his late fifties and is considering taking early retirement so he can attend seminary for three years. His desire is "to be better equipped to continue my role as a layperson involved in ministry."

If the laypeople in our churches matched just a small portion of the ministry of this man, a tidal wave of ministry would flood our churches. Growing twenty-first-century churches will have an atmosphere that will invite the laity to be involved in and to lead ministries. What steps can leaders take today in anticipation of the lay revolution? As always, we begin with prayer.

### 1. Pray for Prayer in Your Church

A praying church is prerequisite for a true unleashing of the laity. Only in an atmosphere of prayer can an atmosphere of ministry develop.

### 2. Guide the People toward Spiritual Gift Discovery and Application

Refer back to the discussion of spiritual gifts in chapter 5. The discovery of gifts is a major facet in liberating the laity for ministry.

### 3. Create an Atmosphere of "Permission" for Ministry.

Let the people know through casual conversations, through sermons, through the testimonies of others, and through written communication that your church is a place where ministry can take place with great freedom. In a church I pastored, our minister of education had a weekly column in our newsletter called "Let My People Go." Each week he highlighted a church member who was involved in ministries. That column sent a message to our members: lay ministry is encouraged and rewarded.

### Refocus on Pastoral Priorities

The role of the pastor has become confused in recent years. Demands of time and energy have increased. And many pastors do not know where their limited time should be used. The Acts 6:4 model, I believe, is the model for pastors. In the apostolic heritage, pastors should devote their time to prayer and ministry of the Word. The latter includes a variety of ministries such as sermon and teaching preparation and equipping ministries, but it does not include being "omnipresent." Growing and discipling churches of the twenty-first century will be those where pastoral priorities are in agreement with biblical standards.

## Evangelism: Don't Just Stand There, Do Something

Conflicting voices confuse church leaders about the way we should be involved in evangelism. Some denominations and parachurch organizations train men and women in an aggressive confrontational model of evangelism. Other church leaders claim that confrontational and cold-call evangelism is ineffective today. Indeed, some of my own early church growth writings repeated the voices of the crowds: cold-call evangelism is out.[10]

Yet, now it appears that our declarations to bury confrontational and cold-call evangelism were responses to culture more than biblical obedience. We were often listening to the wishes of the unbelievers rather than presenting the gospel with urgency and boldness. After all, how many unbelievers, if asked, would really say that they would welcome a confrontation with the claims of the gospel? And while we prepared our funeral messages for confrontational evangelism, studies of church effectiveness in evangelism quietly told us we were wrong. Much to our surprise, the studies indicated a strong correlation between traditional outreach and evangelism models and evangelistic growth in a church.[11]

So what are the implications for churches, particularly those traditional churches that struggle with outreach and evangelism programs that engender little enthusiasm and participation. The answer it seems is to rekindle the fire of enthusiasm for obedience rather than give up on the methodologies. Instead of lamenting about the few who participate, celebrate the few who are there. Do not let discouragement about low levels of participation take away from the blessings God bestows as a result of the faithfulness of a few. Caleb and Joshua (Num. 14:30) and the early followers of Jesus (Acts 1:12–14) certainly attest to the fact that God does not need majority approval to bless His people.

Why does a traditional outreach program correlate positively with evangelistic growth in churches? I believe the answer is twofold. First, the very fact that outreach and evangelism are part of the stated church ministries and programs makes a statement to the church members. It says that the church will have outreach at the forefront of its ministries, that evangelism is eternally important.

Thus it creates an atmosphere that is conducive to outreach. Evangelism becomes a priority of the church.

Second, God blesses our efforts to fulfill the Great Commission. Even when outreach participation is low, God honors the faithfulness of the few. The theme of the remnant of the few is one that runs through the pages of Scripture. Personal blessings will come to those who are faithful; corporate blessings will be bestowed upon the churches.

But a price must be paid. Evangelism is not an exercise in passivity. It requires commitment, time, and personal sacrifices. When Michael Green wrote his concluding thoughts about the church in its early years, he reminded us of the present-day application: "Evangelism was the very life blood of the early Christians, and so we find that 'day by day the Lord added to their number those whom he was saving.' It could happen again, if the Church were prepared to pay the price."[12]

## Understand Your Context for Worship Styles

A considerable amount of energy has been expended on worship services the past decade. This phenomenon has two implications, one negative and one positive.

The positive implication is that worship has taken on new depth. As church leaders have devoted hours of prayer and preparation, the worship services have improved in quality and in the experience of worship. The service, for many churches, is no longer an afterthought, but a deliberately-planned and prayed-for time. The results have been somewhat of a worship revolution in America.

The negative implication is that many Christians have expended their energy fighting and arguing over the "right" style of worship. The churches that reach people in the twenty-first century will spend less time arguing and more time listening. The church leaders will understand that worship style has inherent cultural considerations. The cultural context of the people in the church and the community to be reached by the church will thus influence the style of worship. The worship event can then be both a time for Christians corporately to glorify the Lord and an effective outreach tool to reach seekers with a spirit of joy, worship, and love.

## Plant New Churches

The healthy church of the twenty-first century will be a reproducing church. Failure to start new churches will be a clear sign of illness and church self-centeredness. Church leaders today need to commit to God that they will lead their churches to plant new churches. The method of planting is not the most important issue: traditional, colonization, adoption, satellite, multicongregational, or multicampus. The important issue is that new churches must be started for Great Commission obedience. The dynamic churches of the next century will be in a continuous mode of starting new units year after year.

## The Giant Finally Awakens: The Traditional Church in the Twenty-First Century

God is sovereign. As the simple childhood song goes, "He's got the whole world in His hand . . ." The question is not whether He will have His own way. The question is whether or not we will be a partner in God's work.

This book was written with a prayerful desire to understand the times and, even more importantly, to understand how we should respond to God in these times.

I do believe the traditional church is on the precipice of a great awakening. The signs include the return of values which are often associated with the traditional church: prayer, Sunday School, expository preaching, traditional outreach, and church planting. Such trends do not provide excuses for laziness or lack of leadership. To the contrary, the need for godly, biblical leaders is greater than ever.

Yet while some find comfort in the fact that some traditional elements of the church are returning, the work before us is great. In fact, the task is so monumental that it will be impossible if we strive in our own power. But we serve the same God who promised power to the first church when He gave them the seemingly impossible mandate to evangelize the world: "But you will receive power when the Holy Spirit comes on you; and you will be my witnesses in Jerusalem, and in all Judea and Samaria, and to the ends of the earth (Acts 1:8).

We face a future that is unknown but not uncertain. Our future is certain because of the God who created all of the ages: past, present, and future. That same God promises to empower us to be His witnesses in the days ahead. May you be anointed with His power to serve, to witness, to minister, and to obey.

# Notes

## Introduction

1. See my earlier book, *Eating the Elephant* (Nashville: Broadman and Holman, 1994) which addresses the issue of how to introduce change in a traditional church.

2. Robert Wuthnow, "How Small Groups Are Transforming Our Lives," *Christianity Today*, 38 (February 1994): 23.

3. Ibid.

4. Os Guiness, "Sounding Out the Idols of Church Growth," in *No God but God*, ed. Os Guiness and John Seel (Chicago: Moody Press, 1992), 157.

5. Robert Wuthnow, *Christianity in the Twenty-First Century* (New York: Oxford Press, 1993), 47.

6. Sharon O'Malley, "The Rural Rebound." *American Demographics* (May 1994): 29.

7. Ibid.

8. Leonard Sweet, *Faithquakes* (Nashville: Abingdon Press, 1994), 138.

9. Ibid, 137.

10. Greg Ogden, *The New Reformation* (Grand Rapids: Zondervan, 1990).

11. George Barna, *Absolute Confusion* (Ventura, CA: Regal, 1993), 124–125.

12. Ibid, 64.

13. Ibid, 66.

14. Chip Alford, "Southern Seminary's Mohler Sees New Denominational Era," Baptist Press report, May 25, 1994.

15. Ibid.

16. Ibid.

17. Sweet, 184.

18. Ibid, 184–185.

19. See note 1.

20. Alan L. Wilkins, *Developing Corporate Character* (San Francisco: Jossey Bass Publishers, 1989).

21. Ibid, 9.

22. Ibid, 53–57.

23. Lewis A. Drummond, *The Awakening That Must Come* (Nashville: Broadman, 1978), 93.

24. Glen Martin and Dian Ginter, *Power House* (Nashville: Broadman and Holman, 1994), 2.

25. Drummond, 64.

## Chapter One

1. One possible exception is that of George Barna. In his book *User Friendly Churches* (Ventura, CA: Regal, 1991), Barna devotes an entire chapter to prayer (Chapter 10: "You Do Not Have Because You Do Not Ask"). But even in this overview, the concepts of awakening, renewal, and revival are not tied directly to prayer.

2. Very few church trend books give significant attention to the prayer movement in America. Though not a trend book, C. Peter Wagner's *Churches That Pray* (Ventura, CA: Regal, 1993) is one work devoted entirely to the topic.

3. C. Peter Wagner, *Churches That Pray* (Ventura, CA: Regal, 1993), 18.

4. Keith Hinson, "Revival!" *Facts and Trends*,(November 1993):1.

5. Ibid.

6. Ibid, 4. Emphasis added.

7. Wagner, 23.

8. Ibid, 24–25.

9. Ibid, 25.

10. Earle E. Cairns, *An Endless Line of Splendor* (Wheaton, IL: Tyndale House, 1986), 20–21.

11. Lewis A. Drummond, *The Awakening That Must Come* (Nashville: Broadman, 1978), 14.

12. Cairns, 340.

13. Ibid, 341. Emphasis added.

14. See Thom S. Rainer, *"Prayer: The Power Behind the Principles" The Book of Church Growth: History, Theology, and Principles* (Nashville: Broadman, 1993)

15. C. Kirk Hadaway, *Church Growth Principles: Separating Fact from Fiction* (Nashville: Broadman, 1991), 164. Emphasis in original.

16. Ibid. Emphasis added.

17. See C. Peter Wagner, *Prayer Shield* (Ventura, CA: Regal, 1992) for a full-length book on the topic.

18. Wagner, *Churches That Pray*,. Emphasis in original.

19. Ibid, 169–170.

20. Ibid, 152–153.

21. Neil T. Anderson and Charles Mylander, *Setting Your Church Free* (Ventura, CA: Regal, 1994), 13–14.

22. Ibid, 263–264.

23. Leonard Sweet, *Faithquakes* (Nashville: Abingdon, 1994), 61.

24. Ibid.

25. Cited in Sweet, 61. Emphasis added.

26. Sweet, 63.

## Chapter 2

1. George Barna, *The Frog in the Kettle* (Ventura, CA: Regal, 1990), 118.
2. Ibid.
3. Lewis A. Drummond, *The Awakening That Must Come* (Nashville: Broadman, 1978), 104–106.
4. Ibid, 106.
5. Earle E. Cairns, *An Endless Line of Splendor* (Wheaton, IL: Tyndale, 1986), 319.
6. Ibid.
7. Michael G. Mauldin and Edward Gilbreath, "Selling Out the House of God," in *Christianity Today*, 18, July 1994, 21.
8. William Easum, *Dancing with Dinosaurs* (Nashville: Abingdon, 1993), 14–15.
9. John F. MacArthur, *Ashamed of the Gospel* (Wheaton, IL: Crossway, 1993), 46.
10. "Reformation," in *The Oxford Dictionary of the Christian Church*. Rev. ed. (New York: Oxford University, 1983), 1165.
11. Ron Nash, *Evangelicals in America* (Nashville: Abingdon, 1987), 25.
12. Ibid, 26.
13. Ibid, 27.
14. Ibid.
15. Harold Lindsell, *The Battle for the Bible* (Grand Rapids, MI: Zondervan, 1976)
16. Nash, 99.
17. Ibid, 117.
18. For a thorough history of the Church Growth Movement see Thom S. Rainer, *The Book of Church Growth: History, Theology and Principles* (Nashville: Broadman, 1993).
19. A. R. Tippett, "Portrait of a Missiologist by His Colleague," in *God, Man, and Church Growth* (Grand Rapids, MI: Eerdmans, 1973), 21–22.
20. Among the better sellers by Wagner were *Your Spiritual Gifts Can Help Your Church Grow* (Ventura, CA: Regal, 1979); *Your Church Can Grow* (Ventura, CA: Regal, 1976); and *Leading Your Church to Growth* (Ventura, CA: Regal, 1984).
21. C. Peter Wagner, *Strategies for Church Growth* (Ventura, CA: Regal, 1987), 37.
22. Os Guinness, "Sounding Out the Idols of Church Growth," in *No God but God*, ed. Os Guinness and John Seel (Chicago: Moody, 1992), 174.
23. Ibid.

24. Thomas C. Oden, "On Not Whoring after the Spirit of the Age," in *No God but God*, ed. Os Guinness and John Seel (Chicago: Moody, 1992), 199.

25. Ibid.

26. Ibid, 202.

27. Ibid.

28. David F. Wells, *No Place for Truth or Whatever Happened to Evangelical Theology?* (Grand Rapids, MI: Eerdmans, 1993), 292.

29. Richard L. Mayhue, "Rediscovering Expository Preaching," in *Rediscovering Expository Preaching* by John MacArthur, Jr., et al. (Dallas: Word, 1992), 9.

30. Ibid, 3.

31. This study is cited in Wells, *No Place for Truth*, 251–252. The journals mentioned are *Pulpit Digest* and *Preaching*, covering the time span from 1981 to 1991.

32. Mayhue, 5.

33. Mauldin and Gilbreath, 21.

34. Ibid.

35. Ibid.

36. The reader is encouraged to read the classic work by Michael Green, *Evangelism in the Early Church* (Grand Rapids, MI: Eerdmans, 1970), which supports and articulates this thesis cogently.

## Chapter 3

1. Dean R. Hoge, Benton Johnson, and Donald A. Luidens, *Vanishing Boundaries: The Religion of Mainline Protestant Baby Boomers* (Louisville, KY: Westminster/John Knox, 1994), 185.

2. Ibid, 183.

3. Ibid, see particularly 203–206.

4. Ibid, 176.

5. Ibid.

6. Ibid, 176–177.

7. Ibid, 177.

8. Ibid, 178.

9. Ibid, emphasis added.

10. Ibid, 199, emphasis added.

11. Ibid, 200.

12. William Easum, *Dancing With Dinosaurs* (Nashville: Abingdon, 1993), 101.

13. A good concise summary of the Sunday School movement is J. L. Seymour, "Sunday School Movement," in *Dictionary of Christianity in America*, ed. Daniel G. Reid (Downers Grove, IL: InterVarsity, 1990), 1146–1147.

14. This conclusion has been cited by several. One example is George Barna, *Absolute Confusion* (Ventura, CA: Regal, 1993), 64, where his latest findings are cited: "The rage in church growth cir-

cles lately has been the rush to develop an infrastructure based on a small-group program. Good reasons abound, both theologically and communally, to do so. However, the current study indicates that small groups may have failed to live up to their promise for many people. One out of four adults was involved in a small group between 1991 and 1992. The most recent figures show a decline to just 16% who are involved in a small group that meets for Bible study, prayer or Christian fellowship, other than a Sunday School class."

15. Hoge, et al, *Vanishing Boundaries*, 204, emphasis added.

16. Dean M. Kelley, *Why Conservative Churches Are Growing: A Study in Sociology of Religion* (New York: Harper and Row, 1972; 2nd ed., 1977), 1.

17. Ibid.

18. Dean R. Hoge, "A Test of Theories of Denominational Growth and Decline," in *Understanding Church Growth and Decline, 1950–1978*, ed. Dean R. Hoge and David A. Roozen (New York: Pilgrim, 1979), 197.

19. Hoge, et al, *Vanishing Boundaries*, 181.

20. C. Kirk Hadaway, *Church Growth Principles: Separating Fact form Fiction* (Nashville: Broadman, 1991), 38-56.

21. Ibid, 40, emphasis in original.

22. Ibid, 41, emphasis in original.

23. Ibid, 42, emphasis added.

24. John N. Vaughn, *Megachurches and America's Cities* (Grand Rapids, MI: Baker, 1993), 36.

25. Ibid.

## Chapter 4

1. Leonard Sweet, *Faithquakes* (Nashville: Abingdon, 1994), 13.

2. Cited in William J. Bennett, *The Index of Leading Cultural Indicators* (New York: Touchstone, 1994), 9.

3. Cited in Bennett, 9.

4. Cited in Bennett, 9.

5. Sweet, 13.

6. David Winfrey, "Outreach Almost 'Accidental' as Church Disciples Converts," Baptist Press release, August 8, 1994.

7. Cited in Bennett, 57.

8. Ibid.

9. Cited in Bennett, 117.

10. Ibid.

11. Sweet, 12.

12. Ibid, 12.

13. Os Guinness, *The American Hour* (New York: The Free Press, 1993), 26.

14. Ibid, 27.

15. See Guinness, 82.

16. Guinness, 82.

17. Ibid.

18. Ibid.

19. John F. MacArthur, Jr., *Ashamed of the Gospel* (Wheaton: Crossway, 1993), 148.

20. Ibid.

21. Ibid.

22. Charles Colson, *The Body* (Dallas: Word, 1992), book jacket.

23. Millard J. Erickson, *The Evangelical Mind and Heart* (Grand Rapids: Baker), 45.

## Chapter 5

1. David F. Wells, *No Place For Truth or Whatever Happened to Evangelical Theology?* (Grand Rapids: Eerdmans, 1993), 168.

2. Ibid, 168–169.

3. Ibid, 169.

4. Ibid, 171.

5. Ibid.

6. Ibid, 168.

7. Greg Ogden, *The New Reformation* (Grand Rapids: Zondervan, 1990), 48–49.

8. Martin Luther, "An Appeal to the Ruling Class (1520)," cited in Ogden, 11.

9. Martin Luther, "The Babylonian Captivity of the Church," *Works of Martin Luther* (Philadelphia: Westminster, 1943), cited in Ogden, 11.

10. Ogden, 50.

11. Ibid.

12. Ibid, 51.

13. Ibid, 54.

14. I am using the same terminology that Ogden uses for the title of his book, *The New Reformation.*

15. Ogden, 70.

16. Ibid.

17. R. Paul Stephens, *Liberating the Laity* (Downers Grove: InterVarsity, 1985), 10.

18. Robert E. Slocum, *Maximize Your Ministry* (Colorado Springs: NavPress, 199), back cover.

19. See Lewis A. Drummond, *Leading Your Church in Evangelism* (Nashville: Broadman, 1975), 69–77.

20. See C. Peter Wagner, *Your Spiritual Gifts Can Help Your Church Grow* (Ventura, CA: Regal, 1979).

21. See Ray Stedman, *Body Life* (Glendale, CA: Regal, 1972). Stedman, 81.

23. Howard Snyder, *The Problem of Wineskins* (Downers Grove: InterVarsity, 1975), 83.

24. Ogden, 75.

25. Frank R. Tillapuagh, *Unleashing the Church* (Ventura, CA: Regal, 1982).

26. Ibid, 71.

27. Elton Trueblood, *The Incendiary Fellowship* (New York: Harper and Row, 1967), 41.

28. This biblical study of "equip" was taken from Ogden, 96–116.

29. Ogden, 115.

30. Ibid.

31. The spiritual gift inventory may be ordered from Church Growth Institute, P.O. Box 4404, Lynchburg, VA 24502.

32. Ogden, 11.

33. C. Kirk Hadaway, *Church Growth Principles: Separating Fact from Fiction* (Nashville: Broadman, 1991), 102–103.

34. Ibid, 104–105.

35. For an excellent insight into this period see Michael Green, *Evangelism in the Early Church* (Grand Rapids: Eerdmans, 1970).

## Chapter 6

1. See David F. Wells, *No Place for Truth or Whatever Happened to Evangelical Theology?* (Grand Rapids: Eerdmans, 1993), 220.

2. Ibid.

3. Ibid.

4. Ibid, 228.

5. Ibid, 229.

6. See Thom S. Rainer, *Eating the Elephant* (Nashville: Broadman and Holman, 1994), 97, 99–100, 139,152, 164, 197.

7. Wells, 229.

8. Ibid, 231.

9. Ibid.

10. Ibid.

11. Ibid.

12. James E. Means, *Effective Pastors for a New Century* (Grand Rapids: Baker, 1993), 82.

13. Richard Baxter, *The Reformed Pastor* (Portland: Multnomah, 1982), 5, cited in Means, 82.

14. Mean, 84.

15. Ibid, 84–85.

16. Greg Ogden, *The New Reformation* (Grand Rapids: Zondervan, 1990), 92.

17. C. Kirk Hadaway, *Church Growth Principles: Separating Fact from Fiction* (Nashville: Broadman, 1991), 89.

18. Ibid.

19. See Thom S. Rainer, *The Book of Church Growth* (Nashville: Broadman, 1993), 185–193.
20. Means, 92.
21. Ibid.
22. Ibid.
23. William Barclay, *The Letters to the Galatians and Ephesians, Daily Study Bible Series* (Philadelphia: Westminster, 1956), 171.
24. Stephen R. Covey, *The Seven Habits of Highly Effective People* (New York: Simon and Schuster, 1989).

## Chapter 7

1. *Southern Baptist Handbook* (Nashville: Sunday School Board, 1992), 13.
2. Ibid.
3. One such example is a study I did of 131 churches in the Birmingham (Alabama) Baptist Association in 1993 (the statistics reflect 1992 numbers). I examined the fastest-growing churches by conversion and found that only 19 of the 131 churches had 30 or more baptisms for the year. Two of the nineteen churches were non-traditional. Those two churches had 76 baptisms and an average cumulative attendance of 1,232. Therefore, the two churches baptized one person for every 16.2 persons in regular attendance. The other seventeen churches were traditional. These churches represented 15,010 members and had 1,095 baptisms. The traditional churches baptized one person for every 7.3 persons in regular attendance.
4. See Lee Strobel, *Inside the Mind of Unchurched Harry and Mary* (Grand Rapids: Zondervan, 1993), 13 ff.
5. Ibid, 15.
6. Ibid, 12.
7. Ibid, chpts. 4 and 5.
8. Michael Green, *Evangelism in the Early Church* (Grand Rapids: Eerdmans, 1970), 180.
9. Ibid, 181.
10. Thom S. Rainer, *Eating the Elephant* (Nashville: Broadman and Holman, 1994), 136.
11. C. Peter Wagner, *Churches That Pray* (Ventura, CA: Regal, 1993), 93.
12. Green, 236.
13. Ibid.
14. Ibid.
15. Ibid.
16. Ibid.
17. Ibid, 237.
18. Ibid, 248.
19. Ibid, 249.

20. Ibid, 251. It is ironic that the type of ridicule the subapostolic writers received is similar to that endured by orthodox believers today. Judgement and hell have never been user-friendly topics. Tertullian said, "We get ourselves laughed at for proclaiming that God will one day judge the world."

21. Timothy George, "The Challenge of Evangelism in the History of the Church," in Thom S. Rainer, ed., *Evangelism in the Twenty-first Century* (Wheaton: Harold Shaw, 1989), 14.

22. Ibid, 15.

23. C. Peter Wagner is widely quoted as saying that 10 percent of church members have and will use the gift of evangelism. In my church consultation experience, I have never seen more than five percent of a congregation consistently involved in evangelism.

24. An excellent full-length book on the topic is James Emery White, *Opening the Front Door: Worship and Church Growth* (Nashville: Convention, 1992).

25. See the excellent study of these issues in C. Kirk Hadaway, *Church Growth Principles: Separating Fact from Fiction* (Nashville: Broadman, 1991), 15–37.

## Chapter 8

1. Lyle E. Schaller, *44 Questions for Church Planters* (Nashville: Abingdon, 1991), 15. Schaller's book has a wealth of information about the American historical data on church planting.

2. Aubrey Malphurs, *Planting Growing Churches for the 21st Century* (Grand Rapids: Baker, 1992), 13.

3. Ibid, 14.

4. Ibid.

5. Cited in Malphurs, 35.

6. Malphurs, 36.

7. Cited in Malphurs, 36–37.

8. C. Peter Wagner, *Church Planting for a Greater Harvest* (Ventura: Regal, 1990), 15.

9. Charles L. Chaney, *Church Planting at the End of the Twentieth Century* (Wheaton: Tyndale, rev. ed. 1991), xi.

10. Ibid.

11. Ibid.

12. Wagner, 32–33.

13. Chaney, xi.

14. James Emery White, *Opening the Front Door: Worship and Church Growth* (Nashville: Convention, 1992), 82.

15. Elmer Towns, *Ten of Today's Most Innovative Churches* (Ventura: Regal, 1990), 15.

16. Russell Chandler, *Racing Toward 2001: The Forces Shaping America's Religious Future* (Grand Rapids: Zondervan and Harper, 1992), 299.

17. Larry L. Lewis, The Church Planter's Handbook (Nashville: Broadman, 1992), 18.

18. Ibid.

19. Ibid.

20. John N. Vaughn, *The Large Church* (Grand Rapids: Baker, 1985), 23.

21. Josh Hunt, *Let It Grow! Changing to Multi-Congregation Churches* (Grand Rapids: Baker, 1993), 35.

22. Ibid, 13.

23. Ibid.

24. Ibid, 168.

## Chapter 9

1. David S. Dockery, "Christian Worship: Yesterday and Today," lectures at Canadian Baptist Seminary, April, 1994. The material from these lectures will be included in a forthcoming book, *The Worshiping Church* by David S. Dockery and Lloyd Mims.

2. Steve Miller, *The Contemporary Christian Music Debate: Worldly Compromise or Agent of Renewal?* (Wheaton: Tyndale House, 1993), 109. Miller cites David R. Breed, *The History and Use of Hymns and Hymn Tunes* (Tarrytown, NY: Revell, 1903), 255. The book by Miller is the single best popular work I have read dealing with both historical and contemporary church music. His book was used extensively in this section on a historical journey to worship services in previous ages.

3. Miller, 109.

4. Donald Paul Ellsworth, *Christian Music in Contemporary Witness* (Grand Rapids: Baker, 1979), 30.

5. Karl Gustav Fellerer, *The History of Catholic Church Music*, translated by Francis A. Brunner (Baltimore: Hericon Press, 1961), 56. Cited in Miller, 110.

6. Miller, 100. Originally cited in Jane Stewart Smith, *The Gift of Music* (Wheaton: Crossway, 1987), xix.

7. Fellerer, 56. Cited in Miller, 110.

8. Breed, 290. Cited in Miller, 111.

9. Breed, 38-39. Cited in Miller, 111.

10. Richard Friedenthal, *Luther, His Life and Times*, translated by John Nowell (New York: A Helen and Jurt Wolff Book, Harcourt Brace Jovenovich, 1967), 464. Cited in Miller, 113–114.

11. Ibid.

12. Theodore Hoetty-Nickel, *Luther and Culture, Martin Luther Lectures*, vol 4. (Decorah, Iowa: Luther College Press, 1960), 210. Cited in Miller, 114.

13. *Hymni Luther: animos plures, quam scripta et declamationes acciderunt* (1620), cited by Koch, vol. I, 244; quoted by Hoetty-Nickel, 170. Cited in Miller, 115.

14. H. E. L. Jefferson, Hymns in Christian Worship (New York: Macmillan, 1950), 33. Cited in Miller, 117.

15. Ibid.

16. Miller, 119.

17. Paul David, *Isaac Watts: His Life and Works* (New York: Drydon, 1943), 188-189. Cited in Miller, 119.

18. Miller, 120. Miller cites Donald D. Hustad, *Jubilate! Church Music in the Evangelical Tradition* (Carol Stream, IL: Hope, 1981), 245.

19. Davis, 10. Cited in Miller, 120.

20. David, 212. Cited in Miller, 120-121.

21. Miller, 121.

22. Miller, 121. Miller cites David, 202-203.

23. William Romaine, *The Whole Words* (London, 1787), 990. Cited by Robert M. Stevenson, *Patterns of Protestant Church Worship* (Durham, NC: Duke University, 1953). Cited by Miller, 122.

24. Miller, 125.

25. Ibid, 129.

26. Miller, 130–131. Miller cites James Sallee, *A History of Evangelistic Hymnody* (Grand Rapids: Baker, 1978), 58.

27. Miller, 131. Miller cites Stevenson, 153.

28. J.C. Pollock, Moody: *A Biographical Portrait of the Pacesetter in Modern Mass Evangelism* (New York: Macmillan, 1963), 137. Cited in Miller, 131.

29. Leonard J. Seidel, *Face the Music* (Springfield, VA: Grace Unlimited, 1988), 115.

30. John Bisagno, *How to Build an Evangelistic Church* (Nashville: Broadman, 1971), 71.

31. Hustad, *Jubilate!* 275–276. Cited in Miller, 139.

32. Stevenson, 3. Cited in Miller, 140.

33. Ibid.

34. Dan Peters, Steve Peters, and Cher Merrill, *What About Christian Rock?* (Minneapolis: Bethany, 1986), 196. Cited in Miller, 141.

35. Miller, 141. Miller cites Gordon L. Borrer and Ronald B. Allen, *Worship: Rediscovering the Missing Jewel* (Portland: Multnomah, 1982), 167.

36. Hustad, *Jubilate!* 275-277. Cited in Miller, 141.

37. Ibid, 288. Cited in Miller, 141–142.

38. Ibid, 311. Cited in Miller, 142.

39. Miller, 142–143. Miller notes that Hustad, *Jubilate!* 35, 127, gives a similar evaluation.

40. Donald D. Hustad, "Your God Is Too Small," message preached in Alumni Chapel, The Southern Baptist Theological Seminary, Louisville, Kentucky, September 1, 1994.

41. Trennis Henderson, "Rich Diversity Highlights 'Authentic' Baptist Worship," Baptist Press release, September 14, 1994.

42. Ibid.

43. Melanie Childers, "Worship Styles Found in Kentucky," *Western Recorder*, May 31, 1994, 8.

44. Melanie Childers, "Lexington's Central Baptist Seeks Dignity and Warmth," *Western Recorder*, May 31, 1994, 12. The pastor quoted is Gerald Howell of Central Baptist Church in Lexington, Kentucky.

45. Ibid.

46. Childers, "Worship Styles Found in Kentucky," 8.

## Chapter 10

1. The book to which I refer is Russell Chandler, *Racing Toward 2001: The Forces Shaping America's Future* (Grand Rapids and San Francisco: Zondervan and Harper San Francisco, 1992). Chandler is an award-winning journalist and religion writer for the *Los Angeles Times*. His keen observations and journalistic abilities make this one of the better future-church books in the decade of the nineties.

2. George Barna is the most well known of the survey-research methodologists. His books have made a profound impact on the way we think and do "church." Barna's name became synonymous with the future church when *The Frog in the Kettle* (Ventura: Regal, 1990) was published. He has written a wealth of books in the short time since 1990.

3. Paulus Scharpff, *History of Evangelism*. Trans. by Helga Bender Henry (Grand Rapids: Eerdmans, 1966), 170–172.

4. Ibid, 191.

5. Ibid, 188–189.

6. Dean R. Hoge, Benton Johnson, and Donald A. Luidens, *Vanishing Boundaries: The Religion of Mainline Protestant Baby Boomers* (Louisville: Westminster/ John Knox, 1994), 185.

7. Ibid, see especially 204–206 for the discussion on the Sunday School.

8. Scharpff, 171.

9. Hoge, et al; 178.

10. See Thom S. Rainer, *The Book of Church Growth: History, Theology, and Principles* (Nashville: Broadman, 1993), chapter 22: "Evangelism and Church Growth."

11. See C. Kirk Hadaway, *Church Growth Principles: Separating Fact from Fiction* (Nashville: Broadman, 1991), 15–37.

12. Michael Green, *Evangelism in the Early Church* (Grand Rapids: Eerdmans, 1970), 280.